Our family has witnessed firsthand the love and care La Casa de mi Padre provides for children. We've been privileged to visit and see the extraordinary things God is doing to bring healing and hope for a better future to these kids. In addition to the personal impact La Casa has made on our family, it's been an honor for our organization to partner with them and watch their reach and influence expand even beyond the borders of El Salvador.

– Andy and Sandra Stanley, North Point Ministries

The story of La Casa de mi Padre is a tangible expression of God's goodness and power in this world. Through the obedience of Gary and Sharon Powell and so many others, children in El Salvador and beyond will find hope and healing.

– Eddie Staub, Founder of Eagle Ranch

It's been the fulfillment of a lifelong dream and an honor for our family to invest in the vision of La Casa de mi Padre, where lives are transformed. And there's nothing more compelling than a transformed life. In this book, you'll find remarkable examples of more than one.

– Gary Niebur, President and Co-Founder of
Stan Smith Events

In 2009, our family became connected to the ministry and mission of La Casa de mi Padre and the vision of Gary and Sharon Powell, through a Father/Daughter trip with the Nieburs. We've been enthusiastic supporters ever since. Many times Americans go on mission trips to bring and reflect Jesus to their host organizations, which is a good thing. But with La Casa, it is so much more. We don't go or give to La Casa simply to bring Jesus. We go to La Casa to see God tangibly and visibly at work in the lives of their amazing staff and children. This book wonderfully chronicles the willingness of a few families, the vision and faithfulness of dedicated founders, the support of some amazing friends, and the faithfulness of a very big God.

– Bill Willits, La Casa Board Member; Executive Director
of Ministry Environments at North Point Ministries

D1548183

La Casa de Mi Padre is a true expression of God's faithfulness and his love for his children. The people and provision that have been brought to The Miracle Farm over the years, at precisely the right times, are possible from none other than our Heavenly Father. Gary and Sharon's willingness to say "yes" to the calling and reliance on the Lord's provision are truly acts of faith that are an inspiration to us all.

– Nikki Nixon, La Casa de mi Padre supporter

I believe that if Jesus were to come back tomorrow, he would spend the majority of his time with the children, and the work of La Casa de mi Padre is a reminder to me that "the kingdom of God belongs to such as these." (Luke 18:16 NIV) They seek to create generational change in the lives of families within El Salvador - what a beautiful mission that we can embark on with them!

– Maddie Hooper, Special Education Teacher

I've been on several mission trips to La Casa de mi Padre and each time I go, I become closer to God and make lifelong friends. I've been moved emotionally spending time with the kids of La Casa, too. The Holy Spirit was in us as we prayed, played, and got to know each one. I commend Gary, Sharon, and the whole La Casa staff for the great work they do. It's a wonderful thing for the kids of El Salvador. I thank God for the 70 years I got to spend with my brother, Steve Shugart, who helped me grow closer to God, and introduced me to global(x). I thank Christina for writing this book about a very special place.

– Charles Glenn Shugart

La Casa is a premier illustration of God's servants humbly going where He asked them to go. The children of La Casa experience God's love like they may never have before. Committed houseparents who take care of them, support them and provide structure work hand-in-hand with exceptional staff who reveal Christ through grace, forgiveness and reconciliation with the children's biological families.

– Sam and Liz Jones, La Casa de mi Padre supporters

La Casa is an incredible organization that has raised incredible kids. To partner with them in ministry has been one of the most rewarding experiences of my life. I've had the opportunity to return year after year, getting to know many of the students. The transformations I have seen are beautiful - students coming out of their shells, figuring themselves out, letting go of anger, gaining confidence, seeking God, growing in their faith, and loving each other. La Casa's ministry not only impacts the students but their extended families, and not just now but hopefully for generations to come. God is doing great things through them!

– Kristina Lappin, La Casa de mi Padre supporter
and short-term ministry partner

La Casa de mi Padre is simple in its mission to bring hope and healing to the children it serves, but in carrying out this mission, La Casa's impact is far from simple; it's miraculous and extraordinary. La Casa not only brings hope and healing to the children in its care, but also to the people in its surrounding community; the families of the children in its care; the people who work and live at La Casa as teachers, houseparents and staff members; the people who come to serve La Casa on mission; the people who give to its cause and the people who hear and share its story. When you hear the story of La Casa, you become part of its story and you find hope and healing, too.

– Colleen Jones, global(x) Journey, June 2016

The Miracle Farm

TRUE STORIES OF HOPE AND HEALING AT LA CASA DE MI PADRE

CHRISTINA STEWARD

For Chad, who chooses to love me and
support every dream of mine.

For Gary and Sharon Powell, whose open hands
and hearts have impacted generations.

For the children – past and present – of La Casa
de mi Padre, whose lives are precious to many,
but especially to our heavenly Father.

———

In memory of Steve Shugart (1947–2021),
whose faith was magnetic and who was one of
the most selfless people I've known.

Table of Contents

Preface

THE STORIES TOLD HERE are true to the best of my knowledge. I conducted research, including interviews – in person, via video, phone, and email – to capture details of past events. Some of the various perspectives were combined to reenact stories as a whole, while some are shared in interview format. I also combed through written minutes from meetings held during the early days of La Casa de mi Padre.

My hope is that I covered the key stories within the organization's history. However, there are names and stories that weren't included for one reason or another and, I'm sure, omissions that weren't intentional. That doesn't make them less important. I apologize if I excluded information that should have been included.

Some quotes are paraphrased memories of spoken words and not necessarily the exact words spoken. However, their meaning remains the same. Where possible, for authenticity I left quoted dialogue unaltered for those who speak English as a second language, even if the English wasn't grammatically correct. Some characters' names have been changed to respect their privacy. But, all characters described within these pages are real people who have been a part of the grand story of La Casa de mi Padre.

Introduction

WHEN I STEPPED THROUGH the glass doors and into the October sun, the humidity covered me like a heavy, wet blanket. It was 2014. For a moment, the palm trees lining the sky reminded me of my first home. But the echoes of cars pulling up to the curb and chatter from a chain of passengers winding along the building's exterior snapped me back.

El Salvador hadn't been on my list of places to visit, at least not anytime soon. One night during small group, two of the women were discussing serving on a mission trip through Browns Bridge Church, and El Salvador was one of the destinations. There was a children's home there called La Casa de mi Padre.

"Would you be interested in going?" they asked.

A knot tightened in my stomach. It had been almost nine years since my first and last mission trip. While I was out of the country, a dear friend and her unborn child passed away. I never had the chance to say goodbye. *Mission trip* was synonymous with "loss."

At the same time, I had an inner nudging toward El Salvador. My husband, Chad, and I sponsored a child there through World Vision. It was her pouty face in the photo with large brown eyes that captured my heart so many years before. Hispanic blood ran through my veins, too. And, the last day of the trip would fall on my thirty-eighth birthday.

A few months later, sixteen of us stood curbside at the El Salvador International Airport, waiting for our host. When Gary Powell arrived, he hugged returning teammates and introduced himself to the rest of us. His fair complexion and silver hair stood in stark contrast to the other locals.

"Hi, Christina," Gary said as we shook hands, though I hadn't told him my name.

One by one, we hoisted our luggage through a window at the back of a small bus and climbed on. It was a tight squeeze with floor-to-ceiling suitcases piled behind us. I sat down in a seat made for one and pushed back a curtain that had blocked my view through the window.

Conversation was lively as we rolled down the highway. The terrain was lush – it was the end of the rainy season. Before long, we were surrounded by full industry with supermarkets, fast-food restaurants, and car dealerships. I slowly read billboard signs, trying to piece together the few words I recognized. Cars, trucks, and motorcycles slithered within inches of us, the bus lurching with every tap of the brakes.

Mountain peaks loomed in the distance. If they were volcanoes, I wasn't sure. I secretly watched for smoke, just in case. We stopped to eat a late lunch at Wendy's and then afterward checked into our hotel to unpack and enjoy a short rest.

That evening we drove to Union Church of San Salvador, where Gary was the pastor. The building had a series of steps that led up from the gray brick-paved parking lot to a wide portico. At the top was a side yard filled with vibrant flowering plants and a cactus large enough to hug.

We met Sharon, Gary's wife, who had shoulder-length dirty blonde hair. She flashed a wide, welcoming grin. Empty chairs were arranged in a circle and we each grabbed a seat. A gentle breeze flowed through the archways.

Gary smiled. "Welcome to El Salvador."

For the next couple of hours, the Powells shared about the

culture of the country and gave a brief history of their organization. As I listened, I began to get the sense that La Casa de mi Padre was no ordinary place – that God was doing something extraordinary there. They shared stories of miraculous provision, stories that stirred something inside me.

Later that week our team filed into the tiny chapel that sat high up on the farm. We spread out across the backless wood benches that flanked both sides of the building, with a short aisle down the middle. Gary stood at the front and had just shared stories about the purchase of the land and their plans for the future. The windows were open and a strong, warm breeze rustled the canopy of green leaves.

"Why are you here?" he asked with an inquisitive tone of voice. He slowly scanned the room, locking eyes with whomever was brave enough to look up. His voice softened to just above a whisper.

"Really, why are you here?"

The room was silent. Then, one by one, each teammate shared their personal reasons for being in El Salvador at that moment. It was a time of soul-searching and reflection – a refreshing change from the hustle we were accustomed to in the States.

Then Gary shared his deepest desires for us. That we would see beyond helping the children, though that was a good thing. That we would see God already at work at La Casa and in El Salvador, long before we arrived. That we would personally connect with our heavenly Father.

We ended our time in the chapel with a hymn. There were no instruments or music playing. Only the melody of our voices blending to the words of Amazing Grace.

It set my heart on fire.

Three years later in December 2017, I had just returned from serving with La Casa de mi Padre again – our team helped host their annual Christmas party for their neighbors surrounding the farm. I was unloading the dishwasher and mentally flipping through ideas and goals for the new year. Writing an art-related book had been a fleeting thought, but not one I was taking too seriously.

That's when it happened.

"Christina, I don't want you to share *your* stories yet – I want you to share La Casa's stories," a voice said in my mind and heart.

I froze in place and glanced at the ceiling as if expecting to find something other than white recessed lights. The impression was so strong, emotion pulsed through my body and tears rolled down my face. I wondered if I heard what I thought I heard. I hadn't written a book before.

At first, I didn't share my revelation with anyone but my husband, Chad. A book of that nature was too important – too personal – to rush into on a whim. So, I waited and asked God to show me if I had truly heard from Him. As the days went by, this inner sense of knowing it wasn't my imagination grew stronger. Eventually, I decided it was time to share with Gary and Sharon.

I recorded a short video for them, held my breath, and clicked Send. When I read their reply, goosebumps danced on my skin. Sharon said writing a book had been on their hearts for years, but the timing was uncertain – perhaps a project for when they retired. In that moment, my call to write La Casa's stories met the dream God had given them, long before my dishes went into the wash cycle.

It's because of La Casa's experiences, and the profound impact they've had on my personal faith, that I've written this book – to point to the living God who sees us and cares for us intimately.

Chapter 1

Earthquake

IN THE QUIET OF MORNING on January 13, 2001, Gary asked God if he and his family should remain in El Salvador, where they had lived for the past two years, or return home to Roanoke, Virginia. He had a deep-rooted love for the country, one that started when he was just a teenager. He was confident in his decision to move there, and was now the manager of a luxury hotel in San Salvador. But, was hotel management all that God intended for him there? It was a job he could have easily done in the United States.

God showed him the answer that day, but in a way he never expected.

Later that morning, Gary went to work at the Hilton Princess hotel, located in the Colonia San Benito district. It towered above the capital city with a pristine view of the top of the volcano. Two regal bronze lions stood on pedestals that flanked the front entrance, welcoming guests as they arrived. The doors opened to marble floors, high ceilings, and a grand spiral staircase with iron railing and stone steps. Dark mahogany trim and furnishings accented the cream-colored walls. A formal dining room opened out to the swimming pool area, where a small gazebo with chairs offered a place to relax. Dignitaries often stayed at the hotel.

At 11:30 a.m., Gary was in the office on the mezzanine floor with the controller, Roberto, and their assistant, Evelyn. Suddenly their chairs began to shake. The country sits on the edge of tectonic plates in the earth's surface, so minor tremors are common. Roberto had lived through the 1986 earthquake, though, and his eyes betrayed the ugly truth of what was happening.

The shaking grew more intense as seconds passed. The building lost power. Ceiling tiles bounced above their heads like marionettes on strings. Furniture toppled. The swimming pool drained into the hair salon below. Screams pierced the air and people sprinted for cover.

Roberto and Evelyn braced themselves between the wall and a tall filing cabinet. Gary crawled underneath the desk, preparing to die. Although the hotel was designed to withstand seismic activity, it threatened to collapse at any moment.

Then, after fifty-six long seconds that seemed to last into eternity, it was still.

Gary sprang to evacuate the guests and employees from the hotel. During the earthquake the elevators automatically dropped to the main floor, opened their doors, and locked in place, so everyone crammed into the stairwell. Gary went down the back side of the building and abruptly stopped at the window.

A large ominous cloud rose from inside the volcano. The streets were littered with people. Sirens blared from every direction.

Once the hotel was empty, Gary attempted the drive home, his family the only thing he could think about. But traffic was so gridlocked he couldn't get out of the parking lot. His patience for traffic was thin even on a normal day. So, he opened the door and jumped out. With adrenaline pulsing through his veins, he ran toward the steady incline of the volcano.

Gary splashed through puddles that flung, what looked like, dark ink onto his khaki pants. The water inside the pipes of the hotel sprinkler system had turned black. The sidewalks were congested as he turned onto the street, so he ran down the middle of the road instead. He wove in and out of concrete separators that lined the way. And like a game of Frogger, he dodged traffic that had no concern for pedestrians, everyone on his own frantic mission.

Two miles away, Gary's wife, Sharon, sat outside on the covered patio that ran the length of the house, with two of their kids, Katelyn and Alejandra. There was a table and cabinets that stored craft supplies. Katelyn's birthday was soon, so they were planning crafts for her party.

Suddenly the table shook. At first it seemed like a normal tremor. But the shaking grew stronger. The terracotta roof tiles scraped and clicked against each other.

Sharon swept the girls from under the patio and into the yard. But two of their three boys were riding bikes out front, while little Carlos was asleep upstairs.

She rushed to the door as dishes tumbled from kitchen cabinets and smashed onto the floor, and the TV cabinet crashed down. She yelled for someone to get Carlos.

Whitney, their oldest daughter, was upstairs hanging pictures with help from Ramiro, a driver from the hotel. The Powells had moved into the house only a few weeks prior, so the walls were still bare. A low rumble echoed throughout the house.

"Run, Whitney, run!" Ramiro called.

"The kid! The kid!" Whitney said through her braces.

"I'll get him!" he said.

Whitney bolted down the stairs and flung open the front door. Glass lamps on either side fell and sprayed shards in her path. But she didn't stop. She kept running toward the open, green space across the street.

Carlos was in his crib, one that belonged to the hotel. It had wheels attached to the bottom that allowed it to be moved from room to room. Like a scene in a horror movie, the crib rolled across the floor on its own accord.

At his young age, Carlos had already faced extreme adversity. He was born to a fifteen-year-old girl in El Salvador who couldn't provide for him. So, his aunt took him in. However, she had limited resources herself. When Carlos was just shy of turning a year old, he weighed only nine pounds and couldn't hold his head up. His stomach was swollen and he didn't have the energy to eat the scarce amounts of food available. The Powells first heard about him through a man at Union Church who lived in Carlos's community and was concerned.

They made no promises to the man but agreed to visit the place that Sunday afternoon. When the Powells arrived, Carlos was lying in a plastic woven chair. The aunt said she was just waiting for Carlos to die because she didn't have the means to care for him.

The Powells arranged for their pediatrician to pay a visit, who confirmed Carlos's organs were shutting down. The doctor didn't know if he'd make it through the night.

He did.

Over the course of a month, the Powells nursed him back to health, feeding him every two hours around the clock, using a dropper at first. His weight doubled and he started sitting up and crawling. That was the beginning of a foster relationship between the Powells and Carlos that eventually led to adoption.

By the time Whitney made it to the park, where the whole neighborhood was gathered, the shaking had stopped. She turned around, facing the house. Ramiro came through the doorway holding Carlos in his arms.

Sharon exhaled, her children safely together again. In nervous excitement, they exchanged stories. The boys described the asphalt as a rug shaken out by hand, the normally rock-hard surface rolling in waves. Aftershocks interrupted their conversation, one after another, keeping them on edge. It was impossible to tell if each earthquake would be stronger than the first one. Some of them felt just as strong.

People tried to call their families to make sure they were okay, but calls weren't going through. All eyes were fixed on the volcano where a massive plume of – was it smoke? – rose from inside.

At last Gary stepped onto his home street, the sun high overhead, his face flush. His family was patiently waiting for him, drinking Coke to pass the time. Sharon's blue eyes met his.

He expected her to say they needed to get out of there. That it was time to leave El Salvador.

But instead, she said, "I think we're going to have a lot of work to do."

The earthquake on Saturday, January 13, 2001, triggered a major landslide that caused dust to billow from the San Salvador volcano. The earthquake measured 7.6 on the Richter scale, its epicenter 60 miles offshore of San Miguel, approximately 85 miles east of San Salvador. Hundreds of thousands of homes and buildings were damaged and destroyed. More than 800 people lost their lives.[1]

In the days immediately after the earthquake, the hard work of disaster relief began. Homes were leveled to the ground and people were homeless and hungry. Samaritan's Purse, an international organization that aids the suffering, was present in El Salvador. David Torres, the country director for Samaritan's Purse, frequently traveled in and out of San Salvador to monitor their programs working with local churches. Many nights he went home late, getting stuck in heavy, downtown traffic. So he'd look for alternate routes to shorten the drive. One route in particular worked well even though it was in a suspect part of town with winding, narrow streets.

For several days on this new route, David passed by kids playing in the street. It was the same group each time, children of various ages, even newborns cradled in the arms of older children. Eventually David stopped to meet them. That visit led to a second one. And a third. They'd talk and kick around an old soccer ball. It became a daily routine where he'd park in the street and they would excitedly rush up to his car, barely giving him a chance to open the door. They'd hold on to him and grab his hands, curious to see what he brought that day.

One day, a stocky dark-haired woman joined them at the street. At first she just watched David and the children having their innocent fun. Then eventually she introduced herself. Her name was Sonia and she was watching over the kids.

Although her intentions were good, she lacked the resources to properly care for the children. The older kids wore ragged clothes and few had shirts. The babies were naked. Not even diapers to cover their tiny bottoms.

David was an aerospace engineer with a military background. If you gave him a project with people to lead, he was in his comfort zone. When they placed a baby in his arms and the baby urinated on him, though, he struggled not to gag. He had even had trouble changing his own children's diapers when they were small.

He kept hand sanitizer in the car and doused in it after each visit. But once he became aware of their need, he couldn't turn away. In time he no longer noticed their condition and saw who they were instead – children in desperate need, children loved by God.

Little by little David bought clothes for them, like socks and shoes. He began to help with meals, too. He bought propane for the stove and food staples like rice and beans. He'd visit on the weekends and take them out to play soccer or to the store. David's wife and their own children would visit, too. Over the next few months his family built close relationships with them.

David had limited time and money. If the street kids were going to receive the full care they needed, others had to be involved. So, he shared their story with his men's Bible study group and attendees at Union Church, asking for prayer. Union Church is an English-speaking church in San Salvador, with many expats in attendance.

Gary took a special interest in the children's story. He led both the men's group and adult Sunday school class and, having decided to go and see Sonia's place for himself, invited others from the church to join him.

Among them were Dale and Christy Larson. They had four children – Annalise, Ryne, Erik, and Hans. Dale worked for a multinational food company and was the head of finance operations for Central America. His job had relocated his family from the United States to Costa Rica, Guatemala, and eventually, El Salvador.

There were also Joseph and Jan Napoli. Before moving to El Salvador, they lived in Houston, TX with their two children, Michael and Laura. They were enjoying the house they had built and hosted a Bible study group and Young Life, too.

Joseph worked on the acquisitions team for a major power company and was given the opportunity to relocate to El Salvador, to run business there. But Jan's stomach hurt over that decision. Life was good – why would God ask them to leave home? Weren't they already doing what He called them to do?

Two months later, she unclenched her fists.

"Lord, I don't want to go," she said with tears in her eyes, "but if you want me to, I will."

Her Bible sat open in her lap, with Joshua 1:9 previously underlined on the page. "Have I not commanded you? Be strong and courageous. Do not be afraid; do not be discouraged, for the Lord your God will be with you wherever you go."[2] When she re-read those words, peace flooded her soul.

"Who's in?" Gary asked.

Both the Larsons and Napolis spoke up, as did several others. "We'll go."

Chapter 2

Eyes Adjusting

IN HIGH SCHOOL, Gary became friends with Ricardo, a foreign exchange student from El Salvador. Their friendship led Gary to spend the summer after graduation there, just for fun. One day as he sat in a pizza place, kids peered through the window and begged for food. It was his first real glimpse of need in the world, one that left him wondering how he could be part of the solution. Soon after that summer, El Salvador grew politically unstable until it erupted in a civil war that lasted for twelve years.[3]

During that time, back in the States, Gary and Sharon met and had gotten married. They had four biological children, Whitney, Katelyn, Zach, and Ryan. They also adopted Alejandra from Guatemala.

Alejandra's adoption process was long – it took approximately 14 months to complete – and costs rose higher than expected. DNA tests were required, and her birth mother needed extra hospital care after giving birth to Alejandra. Attorney fees were due. In total, they needed an extra $3,000 to pay off expenses so they could bring their new daughter home. But they didn't have the money.

It was Saturday morning, July 1, 1995. The Powells were scheduled to fly to Guatemala on Monday to pick up Alejandra. Gary was mowing the grass in the front yard. He fervently prayed out loud, his voice swallowed by the rumble of the lawn mower.

"We need you in a big way," he said to God. "You started this. I feel like you were in it from the beginning. I felt like you wanted us to adopt Alejandra. You've provided the way for us to see this through, but God, what am I going to do? We're leaving on Monday and we need three thousand dollars. I don't have it."

As he prayed, Sharon drove up in her van, returning from a visit with her parents. She walked across the yard and handed Gary a sealed envelope. It was from her dad.

Inside, Gary found a check for $2,860 and a handwritten note: "Gary – I had planned to pave your driveway while you were gone, but thought you could use the money more."

His father-in-law didn't know how much money they needed. It was a spiritual marker for Gary, one that encouraged him to have faith to keep going, even when circumstances pointed in a different direction.

Gary managed a hotel and Sharon taught special education preschool. They were rooted in relationships, actively involved with the church, hosted a Bible study in their home, and led short-term mission trips to Central America. Carlos, their sixth and youngest child who was adopted in El Salvador, hadn't been born yet.

In 1998 Gary's hotel changed management and wanted to move him to a different location. They gave him a few options, but none were a good fit personally, so he prepared to look for another job. Then Ricardo called, whom he hadn't spoken to in several years.

"Why don't you come to El Salvador and look for a job?" his friend asked.

That question watered the seed planted deep inside his heart, the memories of his first visit to the country still vivid. Serendipitously, an airline ticket sat on the corner of his desk. They had been scheduled to go on a mission trip, but it was canceled due to an uprising in the community they would be visiting. He called the airline and changed his destination to El Salvador.

Soon after Gary extended the invitation to his friends at church, they made their first visit to Sonia's. It was a Saturday. When they arrived, they drove up to a dilapidated, abandoned warehouse that was more than a hundred years old. Its plaster walls were crumbling down and leaning in, with mud and sticks poking out from underneath. The makeshift door was a large sheet of plywood that was propped against the opening and had to be lifted and shoved out of the way to get inside.

Walking through the door was like flipping off a light switch. There were no windows. The only light source was an exposed bulb that hung from the ceiling. That, and the gaping holes in the roof that allowed sunrays to pierce the cavern inside, revealing a dense cloud of particles swirling through the damp air.

Slowly their eyes adjusted to the darkness. Silhouettes of small bodies formed in their vision, giving way to a new reality.

Eyes in every corner stared back at them.

Suddenly, toddlers with outstretched arms swarmed around the visitors, wanting to be held. Others ran and played and climbed on top of each other. Their skin was dotted with scabies and chickenpox, pus oozing from open blisters. Their heads were crawling with lice.

The exterior walls were exposed, except for a patchwork of dented corrugated metal squares. The kitchen had a small propane stove, but no sink or refrigerator. Rustic wood eating tables filled the cramped space alongside a few dingy white cribs. There were two bedrooms – one for the boys, one for the girls. They slept on tattered mattresses with the foam bursting out, some placed directly on the cracked floor.

They didn't have indoor plumbing. There was a *pila*, though, similar to a laundry room sink found in North American homes but made of cement. It was divided into two sections: a taller water basin and a more open, flat surface to use as a wash area. Water only ran for one to two hours each morning or evening. They would open the faucet while they had access to water, fill up the basin, and use that water for the entire day, or until the water flowed in again. The pila was used to get water for drinking and cooking, washing dishes and laundry, and giving the babies a bath.

There was a broken toilet bowl, a row of white plastic potty-training toilets, lining the wall, to be used instead. Urine and feces smeared the floor.

"I can't do this for very long," Christy whispered to her husband.

"That's all right. Do you want me to tell Gary now?" Dale asked.

"No, but I'll let you know when my time's up."

She glanced over the children until one caught her eye, a baby boy with only a mild rash.

"Can I hold him?" she asked.

They obliged as she took the baby into her arms.

"There's a back yard if you want to go out there," Sharon said.

Christy carried the boy through the door and...stopped. The yard was fenced in, but instead of containing a tidy yard with green grass, there was a heap of trash. Not garbage tied up in scented bags waiting to be collected by the garbage truck. Just waste tossed and left to rot. There were nails, broken bricks, and other rubble from the earthquake, too. It was their dumping ground. And to the children, the cesspool was their playground.

She sat down on the concrete stoop, tears threatening to fall. She sang a melody to soothe the baby, but she needed it just as much. Fifteen minutes passed before she stood up and went back inside.

"Dale, it's time."

He pulled Gary aside, and they exchanged words out of earshot.

"Okay, kids, we need to go," Gary announced without missing a beat.

The group gave their goodbyes and walked outside.

"Please don't go!" the children said, following them to the street.

The kids clung to the cars as if their collective weight would glue the tires down. Gently, the adults coaxed them off. Once the path was clear, they pulled away from the building.

Christy's tears escaped like a violent rainstorm. Slowly the children disappeared into the distance – all fifty-nine of them.

Chapter 3

Moving Day

THE SOUND OF CRYING BABIES with no one to hold them pierced Jan Napoli's heart, so she began to visit each day. The others from the church also made frequent visits during the week and on weekends. Often, they stopped at a market beforehand to buy watermelons or bags of oranges to give the kids a healthy, fresh treat to eat. They held the children and played with them, offering listening ears for the words they eagerly shared. As they spent more time together, those initial feelings of shock and repulsion vanished.

Jan took the children by the carload to the doctor, though she didn't even know all their names. The sickest was a six-month-old boy, so malnourished and weak that he couldn't hold his head up. The pediatrician at the clinic accepted each child, administering shots and medicines as needed.

Their dedication to helping the children was a sacrifice of time and money. Groceries, infant formula, and diapers were all necessities they bought on a regular basis. Yet like David, they knew it wasn't sustainable to only meet immediate needs. They needed a long-term plan.

On occasion the director of the Institute for Protection of Minors, Ismael Rodriguez, visited the Princess Hotel. The hotel was a meeting place for government officials to discuss business, like childcare laws that were rapidly changing at the time. One morning over breakfast, Gary met with the director to discuss what was happening with the children. As it turned out, he was already aware of their situation and had been wanting to shut the place down.

Gary reflected on a book he had read recently: *The Autobiography of George Müller.* Müller was a missionary from Germany who lived in England in the nineteenth century. In 1836, with little money, he opened an orphanage for destitute children.

Müller never asked anyone for money or supplies, but only relied on God to provide for the children. In his autobiography, Müller kept a journal detailing days when supplies, including bread and milk, were critically low. He always turned to prayer, asking God to send someone to help them in their hour of need. Without fail, they'd be contacted by someone who wished to give money, food, or clothing, even if they had little themselves. In total, Müller's orphanage cared for more than 1,100 children[4] through unsolicited funding.

Gary wondered if God would allow *him* to see something like that.

He sought advice from Mr. Rodriguez, to determine how they could legally help the children. So, instead of closing Sonia's place, the director agreed to support Gary and the others in creating an official organization.

On Sunday, December 9, 2001, under the gazebo by the hotel pool, the expats met together to brainstorm next steps. "Guide us," Gary prayed to God at the start of the meeting.

It was important to them not to provide a "gringo" solution.[5] None of them had any experience in running a children's home. They wanted to work with Sonia to help her learn to provide the best for the kids, while at the same time honoring Salvadoran culture. They needed her direct input.

They considered all the costs of operating a children's home, where hiring a trained staff was one of the biggest needs. They needed doctors, caregivers, cooks, cleaners, and someone to handle finances. Physical needs were property, food, clean water, furniture, personal supplies, and play equipment. They scratched a monthly budget of $6,500 on a paper napkin.

"Where are we going to come up with this kind of money?" they wondered out loud. But following God's call and refusing to be afraid, they decided to trust Him to provide the funds.

In the weeks that followed, they held regular meetings to clarify the vision for the home and take action to make it a reality. They hired doctors to give the children medical exams and make recommendations for treatment. They set up an accounting system to track how money was being spent. A foundation had to be formed to legalize the home and allow for US tax-deductible donations. The new school year was about to start, so supplies and uniforms had to be bought for 33 of the school-aged children.

By March 2002 word about their efforts was beginning to spread. A lunch meeting was held with Mr. Rodriguez, from the Institute, to share their specific ideas for creating a children's home. Gary also had lunch with Franklin Graham, President of Samaritan's Purse, where he shared their desire to find a new facility and the hope that the abandoned children would be available for adoption into loving Christian families.

The original vision for the organization was multifaceted. First, a long-term care center would be established outside the city. This center would provide a foster care environment with small groups of children living in individual homes. Each home would have a husband-wife team to serve as foster parents. Second, the children would receive education and life skills training. And lastly, the center would provide opportunities for short-term and long-term missionaries to serve in El Salvador.

A father to the fatherless,
a defender of widows,
is God in his holy dwelling.
God sets the lonely in families.
—Psalm 68:5–6

By May an official organizational board was established. When it came time to choose a name for the organization, Gary read this headline in the local newspaper:

"100 Children Born Every Day without a Father."

The statistic was shocking to him, that so many children were being born with absent fathers. So, the board chose *La Casa de mi Padre* ("My Father's House") for the official name. This name was chosen so that when the children were asked where they lived, they could share that they lived in their "father's house." It was also an acknowledgment that the children's home didn't belong to those who physically established it, but to their heavenly Father.

After researching available properties but still not finding the ideal location, they found a temporary solution – a rental home within walking distance of Sonia's place. The government wouldn't allow students to change schools during the middle of the school year, so a home in the same area was necessary. It would cost $800 a month to rent. Several of the expats signed their names on the contract, making them personally responsible for paying the rent.

The rented house was old but spacious. It had an adequate kitchen, four rooms, and several bathrooms. There was a large central courtyard, with a fountain, that brought in fresh air and light. The roof was flat and accessible – a large space for the children to play.

The house needed work before the children could move in, so they recruited more volunteers. They spent Saturdays scraping the floors and walls, painting, doing repairs, and cleaning. The house needed furnishings, too. It just so happened the owners of a manufacturing business from Taiwan attended Union Church.

"We're closing our facility here in El Salvador. Could you use some bunk beds?" they asked Gary. They also had cabinets, benches, tables, and chairs that needed to go.

"Absolutely, we'll take anything you've got," Gary replied.

They placed several bunk beds in each room. They had cribs built for the babies, and chairs for rocking them to sleep. They set up the kitchen and installed two washing machines and dryers for cleaning laundry. Several weeks later, the house was move-in ready. It was divided by age and sex: babies, small girls, small boys, older girls, and older boys.

A final and most critical detail was to hire a regular staff. After the earthquake Armando Ramírez, the pastor of a small church in Santo Tomás, knocked on the doors at Union Church seeking help. His church building had collapsed to the ground, leaving only the front door standing in its frame. Many in the congregation were injured and left homeless. So, volunteers from Union Church helped them rebuild. Through those relationships, La Casa found workers to cook, clean, and care for the children. Sonia would also move into the new house to continue her role as caretaker.

Moving day was Saturday, May 18, 2002.

The week prior, Alejandro couldn't contain himself. "I'm going to move! I'm going to have a new house! I'm going to have my own bed!" he told his elementary school classmates.

He quickly grabbed his little belongings to take to the new house. Then when he turned back around, he stopped in his tracks. The children were leaving in shifts and he had to wait his turn. But there was solace – the adults brought snacks and drinks to prepare for the exodus.

Government officials were at the new house to help oversee and organize activities. Volunteers were assigned specific tasks to process the parade of children who would march through the doors. One of their main concerns was to keep lice out. So, they set up the first station on the front porch. The porch was lined with metal bars for security.

Step one was to cut hair. Christy gave the boys buzz cuts. No hair meant no lice. But for the girls, buzzes wouldn't do. Long hair was considered a mark of beauty in El Salvador. So, they got the next best thing to buzz cuts: bobs. Hair that fell to the floor was swept up so it never went inside the house.

Step two was shower time. The children stripped on the porch, their soiled clothes placed in garbage bags for washing. Then boys went to their own private bathroom as did girls, where soap and lice shampoo awaited them. For extra accountability, several trusted men went with the boys, and women with the girls, to teach them how to bathe. Most of them didn't even know how to use a bath towel.

After their showers, the kids put on fresh clean clothes. There wasn't money in the budget to buy everyone new clothes, so they found a temporary solution while the dirty clothes were being washed. Dale was an avid T-shirt collector who picked one up everywhere he went. So, each child wore one of his shirts, whether long-sleeved or short, oversized for their tiny body. Then, it was time to pick the girls' hair with lice combs to ensure all the bugs were gone.

Oohs, aahs, and laughter filled the air as the children investigated their new place, bouncing from room to room. They claimed their beds with crisp, clean sheets – a novelty to them. The scent of chicken soup drifted from the kitchen as the staff prepared the first meal in the home.

For a brief moment everyone gathered together. They closed their eyes, bowed their heads, and offered prayers of thanks to God for giving the children a new home – a home that was safe, where all their basic needs would be met.

Processing the children was an all-day affair with unforeseen moments, like when parents knocked on the door at the end of the day. Neighbors had noticed the festivities and let their kids crash the fun. They rummaged to find their children's old clothes and escorted them home with surprise new haircuts.

Likewise, in the girls' room, Jan noticed a child with a buzz cut.

"What are you doing in the girls' room?" Jan asked.

"I'm a *girl*," she replied.

The one who buzzed her head mistook her for a boy, since she had short hair to begin with. She temporarily stayed at La Casa during the daytime. But after that mistake, her mom never brought her back again.

Alejandro couldn't sleep that night. His thick black curls were gone, and he lay sprawled across his new bed that he didn't have to share with anyone else. He was one of four siblings living there now, including his younger brother, Salvador, and two older sisters. To him, it was like a giant family party.

He wasn't the only one awake. Countless children were crying in a loud chorus. Carmen, Hilda, and Loli, three of the hired workers, scurried from one child to the next in order to console them. Some wouldn't have it, though. Even warm baths weren't enough to calm them down.

Carmen was a mom of six – three girls and three boys. Her long dark hair pulled back into a ponytail, accentuated her oval face and prominent cheekbones. She was hired specifically to clean laundry but helped wherever needed.

Hilda was twenty-three years old, petite in stature, with two young daughters at home. She was initially hired to clean, her understanding that she'd be helping out for just that Saturday. But when nighttime fell and there was no one else to leave the kids with, she told her family she wasn't coming home that night.

Loli was a teenager, eighteen years old, responsible for cooking meals. She was familiar with hard work – starting at only five years old, she helped support her family by planting and fertilizing corn in the countryside.

She related to the La Casa children in a personal way – her father had passed away and her mother left. So while Loli had completed third grade, the aunt that raised her wasn't able to send her to school. But she always smiled, in spite of her difficult childhood.

Eventually the children cried themselves to sleep. Before going their separate ways, the expats met at Burger King for a quick dinner. They ordered food at the counter, slumped into their seats, and thanked God for the meal.

When they opened their eyes, they stared at each other across the table. They were a disheveled bunch – they had been in triage mode since 8:00 a.m. that morning. A collective thought lingered in the air.

"What did we just *do*?" someone said, giving voice to it.

They laughed out loud. It was a much-needed stress reliever. But the enormity of the answer washed over them, too. As they reminisced about the day, tears intermingled with laughter. They were out of the boat, just like Peter in the book of Matthew, walking on the water toward Jesus.[6]

The next morning, they went back to La Casa to make a pancake breakfast for the kids. Like a never-ending pasta bowl at Olive Garden, they made stack after stack of pancakes for the fifty-plus mouths that couldn't get enough. A steady stream of sticky, sweet syrup flowed from one plate to the next. They spent most of the day there as the children experienced their first twenty-four hours in the new home. It was rewarding. It was exhausting.

Just two weeks after the children moved out of the old abandoned warehouse, it collapsed from the shake of a strong tremor.

Chapter 4

Fish and Loaves

2003, VIRGINIA

DAWN FORBES SAT ALONE IN HER FAMILY ROOM, sobbing as she watched a promotional video for La Casa de mi Padre. It was her first time seeing the children. As part of a women's ministry, she was helping organize a fundraiser event for mission organizations, where La Casa would be the main beneficiary. Her friend and fellow doctor, Aubrey Knight, had introduced her to La Casa.

Dawn was condensing La Casa's video footage for the event. She played it on loop for several hours straight, growing more and more emotional as the children drew her in.

What...is happening? she wondered. *I'm supposed to be part of this.*

But she didn't know in what way. And the thought of serving outside the United States made her uncomfortable.

She also sensed something familiar about Gary Powell when

she saw him on the screen.

After finishing the video editing, it clicked why Gary was familiar to Dawn – they were old high school friends. But they had lost contact after graduation, more than twenty years earlier.

Soon after the fundraiser, Dawn and her husband, Scott Anderson, were invited to join La Casa's board. Dawn had retired early from her career as a pediatrician, and Scott was a pediatric dentist. She had been rooted in her Christian faith for her entire life, while he became a Christ-follower at the age of forty. And soon after joining the board, they made their first trip to El Salvador.

They spent ample time at La Casa, which included taking care of the kids' immediate medical and dental needs. They also went out into the local community and held medical/dental clinics. They continued this pattern each August for several years.

One morning when their team was leaving the hotel to start the day, there weren't enough vehicles for the entire group. So, Scott and another surgeon volunteered to wait for another vehicle and sat down on the steps outside. Soon after a young man, a stranger, walked by and on hearing their conversation, joined in. He was a third-year medical student, whose dad was a physician. When their ride finally arrived, the young man decided to go with them to the clinic.

When they got there, things weren't going well. There was a grandmother with asthma and she needed to use an inhaler. However, the doctor and several others attending her were having trouble teaching her how to use it. That is, until the medical student stepped up to the plate.

He was already familiar with the inhaler and medication, and spoke fluent Spanish and English. He was able to quickly teach the grandmother everything she needed to know. He was the right person, in the right place, at the right time.

Later that same day, Dawn and her brother, who is an anesthesiologist, were running the unofficial pharmacy. Dawn considered herself a compulsive organizer, fitting for the task. And they had run out of a much-needed eye ointment.

Aubrey's wife, Esther, approached Dawn looking for more.

"There's just none. I promise you," Dawn said. And they both checked to confirm she was right. The box was empty.

Esther left but returned a few minutes later, still hoping for more ointment. She asked if Dawn was sure. Yes, Dawn was sure, as was her brother.

"Let me see if I can find something different." Dawn walked back and peeked inside the ointment box one last time, like closing and opening a refrigerator door, hoping the contents have changed.

This time, however, a single tube of ointment lay inside the box. Only two people had access to the medicine, and neither of them had placed it there.

These personal experiences reminded Scott and Dawn of Jesus, who cared for those in need and fed five thousand people with only five loaves of bread and two fish.[7] Their faith in God deepened. And their relationship with La Casa would continue to grow over the next two decades.

Chapter 5

The Miracle Farm

2004 - 2007

IT WAS TWO DAYS before a La Casa board meeting, and Jan grew unsettled over a major decision the board was about to make. They had found their Promised Land – six acres on which they could build houses for the children to live in families. The only red flag was that sometimes when they visited the property, they were confronted by men who controlled the entrance and exit from the land.

When decision-time came, Jan couldn't shake off the sense of urgency to say no to signing for the land. And soon she'd find out why. The board was informed that the property they were considering was located right in the middle of gang-territory.

They had scouted more than twenty different properties in search of the right one. The ideal property would have twenty to thirty acres of land, allowing multiple homes to be built alongside other supporting buildings, like an office. It would be in a rural setting without heavy traffic and have ample space for the children to run and play. Another consideration was that in areas protected by the government, they could only build on 20 percent of the land.

The closer the property was to San Salvador, the higher the price. Some options were ruled out based on price alone. Another property they considered had forty-plus acres of land and was within budget, but was forty-five minutes away from the city – too far from hospitals and other important facilities. Then one day Gary received an email from the son of an attorney who owned property in Santo Tomás.

His father, Dr. Zaldívar, bought a coffee farm during the 1950s, just ten miles outside of San Salvador. There were two farms, actually – the original one plus an adjoining farm that was purchased later. Together they sat on forty-two acres of land and were still working farms with hundreds of coffee plants, orange trees, and coconut trees. There were only a few small houses on the land that were used by the caretaker, but aside from that it was undeveloped. The attorney wanted to sell the farm for a reasonable price. So, it became La Casa's number one prospect for future land development.

There was a knock at the door.

"Are you Gary Powell?" asked a man standing outside Gary's office at the hotel.

"Yes, how can I help you?"

"My name is Dale, and I understand you have a children's home." Dale was a frequent, long-term visitor of the hotel who lived in California. "I'd like to hear about it, if you don't mind."

They sat down together while Gary shared about La Casa. After they talked for a while, Dale asked another question. "Would you mind if we went down to see the children?"

Gary's schedule was flexible. "Sure, let's go down and see the kids."

Some of the children were at school, but many were home. Babies were asleep in their cribs, toddlers played with toys, and others swung on the swing set. Dale met the La Casa staff, too.

"You mentioned you were looking at property," Dale said. "If you have time, can we go look at it, too?"

They drove to the farm nestled in Santo Tomás. It was the rainy season and the land was cloaked in green. They traversed a narrow unpaved road that wound through the property and stopped at different points to observe the scenery. The road ended at the highest elevation, which provided a panoramic view of the treetops on one side and Lake Ilopango on the other, approximately one mile away from the farm.

A humble house sat at the top. They walked behind it and peered toward the lake in the distance. A gentle breeze brushed their faces. It was tranquil.

"Let's just pray," Dale said.

The two men prayed together, asking God to lead La Casa to the right property, to show them what to do with the land they stood on. They asked for wisdom to know if it was the right place and if so, when to buy it. They prayed it would be a place of healing and restoration for the children. When they finished praying, they drove back down the hill.

"How much is the property?" Dale asked.

"It's one hundred seventy-five thousand dollars," Gary said.

"How does that work in El Salvador?"

"Well, you sign a *compraventa* with someone, which is like a promissory note. You put down 10 percent of the purchase price and then beyond that, you make payments on it, whatever you agree upon, with the owner of the property."

Dale said, "I'll give you a check tomorrow morning."

Gary's draw dropped. That night he shared about his time with Dale with the La Casa board. They agreed it was God's leading and that they should move forward if Dale followed through on his promise.

The next day, he slid a $17,500 check onto Gary's desk.

In August of that same year, Gary met with Dr. Zaldívar. He shared La Casa's vision for the land, which was pleasing to him. They created a document that stated La Casa had one year to pay for the land in full, given they had the first 10 percent in hand.

Over the next year donors gave money toward the land. There were small gifts and large gifts alike, each dollar bringing them closer to their dream. One day when a medical team was serving with La Casa, one of the doctors placed a folded check in Gary's hand and said it was for the land. When Gary went up to his office, he opened the check. It was $25,000.

Just ten days before the final payment deadline, La Casa was still short $109,500. Gary was getting ready to fly to England for a work conference with Hilton and wouldn't be back until after the deadline passed. He emailed La Casa's board asking them to pray that God would provide the remaining funds. Because if they didn't receive them, they would lose the money they had invested.

Gary received replies back from the board, including one from Joseph Napoli. Joseph suggested Gary go to the bank to borrow money so they could pay off the land on time, using the property as its own collateral. But with his immediate travel plans, it was impossible to go to the bank.

Gary lifted his own prayer to God.

"God, I know you started this process. But we need you to help us. Because I can't see the end. I can't see how this is going to happen."

Gary flew overnight and landed in London the next day. He was never able to fall asleep on airplanes, so he hadn't slept at all. He checked into the hotel and set up his computer.

Among his emails was one from a La Casa board member, who said La Casa had just received two checks in the mail for the land: one for $450, the other for $50,000.

Gary wrote in his journal that day. "God, You are showing us and teaching all of us a BIG lesson in who You are! Go for it! Yes Lord, blow our minds and leave us dumbfounded! May we all come away from this having grown our faith and trust in You."

After the conference was over Gary flew back to El Salvador with a connecting flight in Washington, D.C. Aubrey Knight, another La Casa board member, had recently relocated to D.C. from Roanoke, so they met to have breakfast during the layover.

"Has any more money come in for the land?" Gary asked.

Aubrey grinned.

"Yes, it has," he said. There was a donor who received a check after leaving the company he worked for. The company had established an account for him that was accumulating money – and he had no idea about it. Or at the least, had forgotten about it. He endorsed it over for the purchase of the land.

"Wow!" Gary said. "So where do we stand?"

"We only need sixteen thousand dollars."

"Okay, let me contact Dr. Zaldívar and see if we can give him what we have. And if he'll give us extended time on our agreement to finish paying it off."

So Gary appealed to the attorney. He accepted their offer and collected the money they had already raised. Then he gave them extra time to provide the rest.

When Gary returned home to El Salvador, he received another email from Aubrey. La Casa had received an unexpected stock donation.

Many years prior, the stock donor had purchased penny stock for $0.10–$0.12 per share. He was an amateur investor at best. When the stock price increased to $0.25, he considered that too expensive and quit buying new shares. The stock became an afterthought for years.

Then one day while he was at church, a man spoke about donating stocks for charitable purposes. That talk prompted him to check the value of the penny stock. The price had soared to $80. A friend of La Casa's, he suddenly realized he was sitting on the money that they were hoping for.

Turning stock around was an unfamiliar process to La Casa. But when it sold, it was for $22,000, just what they needed to finish paying for the land, including closing costs.

When La Casa de mi Padre received the land deed, they found several references to *Finca El Milagro* ("Miracle Farm") on it. Dr. Zaldívar had given the farm that name when he bought it, and registered it with the mayor's office. Official maps of Santo Tomás indicated Finca El Milagro.

While they were cleaning out an old storage building on the property, they discovered a hanging sign tucked inside. The words "Finca El Milagro" were scripted in metal, a sign that hung on the gate at the front entrance once upon a time. The letters were weathered and rusted. A beautiful relic, they tucked it away for another day.

La Casa held a ceremonial signing of the deed, where they met in the tiny house that overlooked the lake. The children were given a document to sign so that they felt like they were taking ownership, too. Gary asked if any of them would like to say something.

To everyone's surprise, Silvia stood up behind the microphone. She was not yet a teenager, with a quiet nature. With poise many didn't know she possessed, she thanked God for giving them the farm – what would eventually become their new home.

Then she looked into the eyes of the audience. "Thank you for not forgetting us."

Early one Sunday morning, David Torres unexpectedly dropped by Gary and Sharon's house. It was a typical Sunday – the Powells were preparing for church and visiting La Casa, where they'd share a Bible story with the kids and enjoy lunch together. In the evening there would be a Bible study group that David and his wife attended, too. They had made pancakes so they invited David in for breakfast.

"There's a donor, through Samaritan's Purse, who wants to build a church," David said.

"Yeah?" Gary said.

"Maybe we could build a church on the property out there."

"That sounds cool."

"We can come up with a proposal to submit into the system." Proposals from across the world were being considered.

Gary agreed, and later they drove out to the property to find a spot to build the church, should it be granted to La Casa. They eyed a hill just inside the entrance. For the amount of money being offered they couldn't build anything large, but a small structure on top of the hill could work. It could be a symbolic lighthouse to greet everyone who entered the property.

It was hot outside as they climbed the hill on foot. There was no path as they traipsed through overgrowth that was waist-high. They struggled to get up to the very top – it was steep and slippery. But when they finally made it they looked down across the land. It was perfect.

David climbed up a tree and tied a scrap of cloth around one of the limbs. He maneuvered his way back down.

"We've marked our spot," he said.

Soon afterward they created the proposal. Their idea was to build a small chapel atop the hill. The chapel could be used for prayer, for meeting with the La Casa kids, and for special occasions. David submitted their proposal.

Several weeks passed. Gary hadn't thought about the proposal much. Then David paid another visit.

"We got it," David said.

"Excuse me?" Gary said.

"We got it. The donor wants to build a church here."

"Are you serious?"

"Yes."

Gary had a contact who owned an architectural design firm, whose husband owned a construction company. She had completed work for the hotel in the past. So Gary asked her to draft ideas for the chapel.

The first drawings she sent showed a structure with a lot of glass – a kind of crystal cathedral. But they wanted architecture that would fit better into their rural setting. A design that would be the model for other buildings eventually built on the property.

There was a back-and-forth of designs until they agreed on a solution, one that was less crystal cathedral and more Santa Fe. The chapel would be built from block and have arched windows on the sides. A single larger arched window would accent the back wall. The front doors would be modeled after older ones they spotted in Antigua, Guatemala – arched double doors that opened straight into the chapel.

At the same time there was a young pediatric nurse named Lydia Holmer, who had worked with La Casa for a year. Her friends and family called her "Puschel." The children at La Casa were drawn to Puschel – she outwardly loved others and was an encouragement to everyone she met. But while in El Salvador she started experiencing severe pain, causing her to go back home to Germany. There she was diagnosed with cancer.

La Casa stayed in touch with her.

"Is there anything you think would be really cool to see in the chapel?" Gary asked Puschel..

"What about a bell tower?" she said. "If you build the tower, I'll have a bell made that fits inside."

Before Puschel traveled to El Salvador, she had created a website to keep her friends updated on her work at La Casa. It was through this website that she was able to quickly raise money for the bell, which her family would ship to El Salvador when it was complete.[8]

So, the bell tower was added to the construction plans for the chapel. Puschel would have Ephesians 6:10 engraved on the bell: "Finally my brothers, be strong in the Lord and in his mighty power." It would ring across the property and into the surrounding community.

Construction for the chapel began just six weeks before a planned "summit" meeting for La Casa. Their goal was to have the chapel finished in time so it could be inaugurated during the event. But it wouldn't be easy.

Because there was no road to the top of the hill, the building materials had to be carried on the workers' backs. They hoisted cinder blocks, along with bags of cement, sand, and gravel. Steel had to be manually lifted, too.

Gary often visited the construction site with the project manager from Samaritan's Purse.

"Are we going to make this deadline? We've got a lot of work," Gary said to him.

They often brought soft drinks or cake to encourage the workers. Gary would share with them the vision for the land and what would take place inside the chapel. And after working long days seven days a week, the building was finished in time for the inauguration. The only thing missing was the bell.

Several months later, when it arrived at Finca El Milagro and was hung in the chapel, they rang the bell for the first time. Gary recorded its sound and sent it to Puschel. It made her so happy, she placed the recording on her website for others to hear and to thank her friends for their support.[9]

As her cancer progressed, Puschel never returned to El Salvador. She passed away five years later at the age of twenty-eight. But her legacy continues in many ways, including Gary re-telling the story of her contributing the bell, whenever teams visiting La Casa gather inside the chapel.

Chapter 6

Shake It to the Core

2006

"HOW DO YOU get that deep, deep faith?" the reporter asked Gary. A local newspaper was interviewing him.

"By experiencing things that shake it to the core," he said.

While they were still talking, his phone rang. It was Sharon. She was frantic.

Whitney was home from college on Christmas break and didn't see the delivery truck barreling toward her. She had spent the day at La Casa and was being dropped off in front of her house late that afternoon. She stepped to cross the street as the children shouted and waved goodbye behind her. She turned around to wave back.

The truck slammed into Whitney at full speed and dragged her limp body forty-five feet across the pavement before it stopped. Sharon had just arrived home and rushed to Whitney's side. Whitney was pinned underneath the vehicle.

Friends and neighbors also sprang into action and with many hands defying the weight of the truck, they lifted it from Whitney's body. She was still, pale, and shrouded with blood. And then, she woke up.

Whitney screamed in pain. Medical professionals arrived and carried her to the hospital by ambulance. She was subjected to X-rays, CAT scans, and MRIs to assess the extent of her injuries. She suffered broken vertebrae in her lower back, a broken tailbone, and a laceration that stretched from her eye, across her forehead, and to the back of her head. She had third-degree burns on her left arm, seared by the truck's muffler. And, she had severe abrasions across her back. Her cell phone was in her back pocket at the time of the accident and was bent into a V shape.

The police brought the driver to the hospital. There, the officer wanted Whitney to sign paperwork regarding the accident. Gary explained to the officer that, given her condition, she wasn't able to sign anything. So, the officer said the driver would go to jail.

In El Salvador when someone sheds blood, that person automatically goes to jail, even if it was an accident. Just as Whitney didn't see the truck before impact, the driver didn't see Whitney crossing the street, either. He never had time to react.

However, there was one thing that could save him – forgiveness. The Powells chose not to press charges and convinced the police to let the man go. Then they walked outside of the emergency room and spoke with the driver, who was trembling. They prayed with him.

For several days after the accident, family and friends gathered together and prayed that Whitney would live.

She did.

2008

The weight of the global financial crisis pressed on the shoulders of La Casa de mi Padre. La Casa depended on financial donations for their operating budget, and donations were down severely. In November of that year, they faced a pivotal moment.

Gary was working in his office when his administrative assistant, Evelyn, entered the room. She said that checks needed to be written for food and medicine for La Casa, and she needed Gary's advice. He was puzzled. So, she explained that the food was going to cost $600 and the medicine, $280. But there was only $1.62 in the bank account.

For a moment, Gary was speechless. Then he said, "Evelyn, give me a minute."

He left his office and stepped outside onto the terrace of the hotel. A sofa leaned against the cream-colored wall and he sat down on it. He lifted his head to the clear blue sky, where only a few puffy white clouds drifted by.

"Father, I don't know what to do," he prayed. "The kids need to eat, and we need to buy medicine for them. I can't even go back in and talk to Evelyn about it, until I know what to do. I ask you to intervene. I ask for wisdom. I'll just sit here until I know."

So there he sat, alone in the quiet, and waited for an answer. Fifteen minutes passed.

I need to get back to work, but Father, I need an answer, Gary thought.

Then, he heard an inaudible but still, small voice. Write the checks. I'll cover them, the voice said.

Then Gary stood up, walked back inside, and stopped at Evelyn's office. "I don't know how, but just write the checks," he said to her.

"Okaaay," she said hesitantly.

He raised his finger and said, "Mark my word. God will cover those checks."

So she did as he asked. Then he signed the checks and placed them on top of his desk. Later that afternoon the director of La Casa visited his office. He handed the checks to her.

"Right now we only have one dollar and sixty-two cents in the account. But I want you to go to the bank tomorrow and cash them," he said. "They'll be covered." She typically arrived at the bank at 10:00 a.m., one hour after they opened. There was a cushion of time, even if a very small one.

The next morning Gary was eating breakfast with a friend from Florida, who was a wealth manager. The man had been involved with another ministry and also gave to La Casa on occasion. Gary was certain God would use his friend to cover the checks.

But as Gary watched the clock, it drew closer and closer to 9:00 a.m. Then his friend stood up to leave. Gary's stomach tightened.

Oh no, Lord, how's this going to happen? Gary thought.

As he said goodbye to his friend, the phone in the hotel restaurant chirped.

"The phone's for you," the head waiter said to Gary.

Gary grabbed the phone, where Evelyn was on the line. "There's a couple up here from Atlanta that has dropped by to see you," she said. "They only have a minute because they have to catch a plane."

"Okay, send them on down," Gary said.

When they appeared in the lobby, it was a married couple who had lived in El Salvador and were once part of Union Church. They had owned a small gym and held exercise classes for the

La Casa kids. It had been years since Gary had seen them.

"We sold the gym," they said. "We netted four thousand dollars, and don't know why, but we keep hearing God say to give you this one thousand dollars." They handed him cash.

Tears rolled down Gary's face. It was enough to cover the food and medicine, with extra to buy Thanksgiving dinner for the kids, too.

Chapter 7

The Bridge

2011

EL SALVADORAN LAW STATES THAT once a child turns the age of eighteen, they can no longer live at La Casa. By 2009, La Casa had a handful of children close to that pivotal age. But unlike the United States, where children often start independent life at eighteen, young adults in El Salvador remain with their family until they start a family of their own. So, the La Casa board was in deep discussion about how to handle the aging out process, especially since their children didn't have another safe place to call home.

One day a man, Mr. Doño, knocked on the door at La Casa. He owned a home in Planes de Renderos, approximately thirty minutes from San Salvador by car. He was a successful businessman and used the home to help others in need. The home was vacant and he was searching for a ministry that might need it, leading him to La Casa. He asked a lot of questions but at the end, simply thanked Gerardo – the house dad – and left.

Several days later La Casa received a phone call. To their surprise, Mr. Doño offered the vacant home to them, rent-free. So, Gerardo and Gary planned a visit to see it.

When they arrived, they opened the front door at the bottom level. Brown, crunchy leaves stacked ten inches deep were shoved aside. They carefully climbed up exterior stairs to enter the main home. Inside there were broken sinks and windows, and cracked toilets. Thick dust blanketed every surface.

The layout of the home was awkward. There was a large room added onto the front porch that could only be accessed from outside. The home also stood close to a busy, curving highway. There wasn't much parking space, and you had to watch carefully for oncoming traffic when entering and exiting the home.

After seeing the space, Gary needed time to consider the offer. Three weeks passed before they paid a second visit to the home. This time, the house had been cleaned up some, with the leaves and debris cleared away. It was easier to envision the house in working order. But even rent-free, the house would cost La Casa over $3,000 a month to maintain. It was a serious investment, given there were still months when they struggled to cover operating costs.

Another several weeks passed before they met with Mr. Doño again. His office was in Santa Elena, inside a two-story building. On the first floor was a distributorship where he sold tires, brakes, and other parts for cars. The offices were on the second floor.

Gary and Gerardo sat downstairs in the waiting room. They were alone, with the exception of two women, who didn't stay for long. After the women left, Gary shared his heart.

"I don't feel at peace about a lot of this stuff," he said.

So, they prayed.

"God, show us Your will. Help us to see. With whatever Mr.

Doño says, give us a clear answer to what we're supposed to do."

They walked upstairs and sat down in the office. It was a tight space – their backs were against the wall with Mr. Doño's desk immediately in front of them.

He shared why it was important to him that he help others, reflecting on his own challenges when he was younger. Then, he moved on to the reason for their meeting.

"You boys take a long time to make a decision," he said. "I'm not going to rent the house to you."

The house had been broken into. A criminal removed the bars from the window and damaged the inside. Mr. Doño had to post twenty-four-hour security there.

There's our answer, Gary thought. But it wasn't the end of the conversation.

"I'm going to donate it to you," Mr. Doño said.

Neither Gary nor Gerardo were sure of what they heard. So, they asked him to repeat his statement.

He picked up a set of keys from his desk and handed them over.

"I'm giving you a house. My granddaughter has the deed on her desk. Take it to your attorney, have them prepare the transfer of ownership, and I'll sign it. It's yours."

They took the deed and walked back outside to their car. Gary climbed into the driver's seat with Gerardo on the passenger side. For a few minutes, they just sat there and bawled.

The property was assessed at $125,000, and La Casa made sure there were no leans against it. They brought the deed to their attorney, who drew up papers, and the property was signed over to them.

Soon after, a team from North Point Community Church in Atlanta was sent down to help restore the house to working order. One of the team members was an interior designer who suggested ways to make the home both functional and beautiful. They tore down a wall that divided the living room from a breakfast nook, and created an open study area. They painted over old wall paneling that was covered with gold flying geese.

The Hilton Princess hotel donated beds to place in the home. They also repaired broken windows, replaced cracked sinks and toilets, and painted walls.

The first group of young adults, who had aged out of La Casa, moved into the new "transition" home, nicknamed the "Bridge." It was a place designed for them to live independently, while in a family-like setting with their housemates. La Casa placed resident assistants in the home – one to help guide the young women, and one to guide the young men. It was a place to thrive.

Chapter 8

Sting

WE OPENED THE dark-brown double doors at Union Church and stepped into the sanctuary. Just hours before, the old wooden pews had been full, the sounds of acoustic worship music and a spirited message from Gary filling the air. Now you could only hear the scuffle of our shoes on the tile floor. It was May 2018, and I was in El Salvador for the week, collecting stories for the writing of this book.

"My house shall be called a house of prayer for all nations. Isaiah 56:7" was hand-lettered on the back wall. At the front was an almost floor-to-ceiling A-shaped window that, when you stood at the right vantage point, perfectly framed the picturesque volcano. A few puffy clouds shrouded the mountain top.

We entered a small room nestled just off the sanctuary – Gary's office. It was brightly lit, the sun filtering through a window with large glass panes that were cranked open. It was quiet except for the bird songs that carried through the window.

Gary sat at his desk and I on a seat on the opposite side of the room. His black-rimmed eyeglasses and dark Vans reminded me of a college professor. I grabbed my voice recorder – a necessity so I didn't have to rely on my not-so-great memory. I hoped it wasn't too distracting.

"Can we just pray before we get started?" Gary asked.

"Yes, please do," I said, wishing the thought had already occurred to me.

We said amen and shifted in our seats. A few seconds of silence followed. Then I pressed the red button on the recorder.

He recounted the day of the earthquake and how those on the coast reported the tide going out and not immediately coming back in. So, there were tsunami warnings on top of the mass chaos caused by the quake. He smiled and snickered softly when he talked about finding his family at the park waiting for him.

"Those early days were unbelievable. That first day was scary, to say the least," he said in reference to moving the children from Sonia's place. "We were all emotionally fragile." A pregnant pause. "Scared." Another pause. "Challenged."

I learned early on that Gary was a gifted storyteller. He transported the listener right into the scene he narrated, making them visualize what he saw in his mind. Making them feel what he felt.

Soon after La Casa de mi Padre officially opened their doors, they began to get visitors in the evening – women who worked as prostitutes – to pick up their children.

"I remember feeling so surprised," Gary said. "Why were these people coming by? What is going on? And that's when we discovered that Sonia had actually set up a business – babysitting these children and charging these moms thirty dollars a month. So, these kids weren't necessarily orphans."

This discovery left La Casa in a pickle. Suddenly they had children under their roof who had families after all. So, they gave those families time to find alternative care. When that process was complete, La Casa's population went down from fifty-nine children to six. Only the true orphans remained. Sonia was no longer working at La Casa, either.

With the new vacancies, La Casa began working with the government to bring in more children. They accepted handfuls of children at a time, getting them settled into the home before bringing in more. Eventually the number grew back to forty. Most of them had been living in extreme poverty, their families unable to care for them.

More sibling groups were received, including one group of six. There were also two sisters, Diana and Marina, from a different family. Diana was eight years old and Marina, eleven.

The Institute for Protection of Minors required that family members be able to visit their child at La Casa periodically. So, La Casa organized a Family Visit Day once a month. The family would visit with their children on the front porch of the house, while the rest of the kids stayed inside.

"These relatives would bring them soft drinks like Cokes and maybe a bag of cheese puffs, and they would just look at each other," Gary said. "They had no idea how to interact." Meanwhile inside the house, some of the other kids would get jealous that no one was there to visit them. Gary confessed his attitude about family visits wasn't the best back then, recognizing the challenges that stemmed from improper child care within the families. "I had wished they would allow us to have full access to the children and they would just step out of their lives," he said.

Diana and Marina had lived at La Casa for several months, and no one ever came to see them on Family Visit days. Then one day, the government notified La Casa that the girls were being adopted. The adopter was an older woman who lived in the States. She was a widow who spoke no Spanish and little English. In La Casa's eyes it wasn't a good cultural match for the girls, but they had no control over the adoption.

La Casa threw a goodbye party for Diana and Marina. During the party a strange man, woman, and little boy walked in. The girls' eyes grew large.

Recognizing their connection but not fully understanding, Gary asked them who the people were. He was shocked to learn it was their aunt, uncle, and younger brother.

Diana and Marina clung to their brother, now wishing they could stay with their real family. If only La Casa had known they had family, they could have prevented the adoption. Likewise, if only the family had known about the girls' situation, they would have been involved, they said. But it was too late. The adoption was done.

That was the sting that started to change the way La Casa viewed their role in the children's lives. Two other events that followed lodged the stinger even deeper. The first happened an hour's drive northeast of Atlanta, Georgia.

In 2006, four years after the children were moved to La Casa de mi Padre, the organization was getting by but lacked solid structure.

"We were just fumbling along and trying to follow the rules and do the best we could with what we had," Gary said.

That's when Gary met with Lily Colgate, who was the founder of International City of Refuge, a non-profit in El Salvador that helped the orphaned and abandoned. Lily shared that she attended a seminar in the States about how to establish and run a children's home. It was just what La Casa needed.

Lily gave Gary the name of her contact, Annette Ryan at Eagle

Ranch in Georgia. Eagle Ranch was an established children's home that had the same vision as La Casa – to care for children in need within family-like settings. Annette was part of Eagle Ranch's Wings Initiative program, which gave guidance to other children's homes just getting started or in need of change.[10] Gary called her to introduce himself and ask about attending their next seminar, only to find that she already knew who he was. Eagle Ranch was working with another home in El Salvador and found La Casa through their own research.

Their next seminar wouldn't be for another six months, she said. It was a long time to wait, but Gary accepted that and hung up the phone. A short while later, La Casa's phone rang. It was Annette. This time, Eagle Ranch extended a special invitation to La Casa's board members to visit them in Georgia and show La Casa how they operated.

Soon after Annette, Ronnie Weeks (the lead counselor at Eagle Ranch), and Eddie Staub (its founder) met with Gary and the others inside the Eagle Ranch boardroom. With Diana and Marina's adoption still fresh in the minds of those from La Casa, Eagle Ranch shared, based on their own experience, the need for La Casa to have contact with the children's biological families. The children needed counseling, too, a vital component missing from La Casa's current model.

"There were a lot of tears," Gary said.

The second paradigm shift happened back in El Salvador. La Casa held a "summit" meeting, where many of the people involved with La Casa were invited. The goal was to create a master plan, in light of what they learned at Eagle Ranch, for moving forward in each of the specific areas of the organization. The La Casa children were there, too.

During the summit the children were given the opportunity to stand up and share what La Casa meant to them. One little boy's response caught them off guard.

"I just wish I could see my dad and my brother and sister," he said through tears. Both his parents were in prison for selling drugs. His siblings were in the States with relatives.

His confession then started a chain reaction with the rest of the kids. They, too, wished to be with their fathers, or mothers, or aunts and uncles. Up to that point, La Casa hadn't worked with the relatives at all, to prepare them for caring for the children. If the kids were going to have the family connections they craved, that had to change.

La Casa's first meeting with Eagle Ranch was just the beginning of what would become an intense mentor/mentee relationship that spanned years. La Casa completely adopted Eagle Ranch's model for their organization. That included a therapeutic program with a fresh focus on families – including the children's biological ones.

Chapter 9

Hope

"Whoever finds their life will lose it,
and whoever loses their life for my sake will find it."[11]

LA CASA WAITED TEN LONG YEARS from the time they purchased Finca El Milagro to when they secured building permits, raised money to complete the build, and saw their dream of living at the farm become reality. In 2015 they moved the children into two separate homes on the farm – one for the boys and one for the girls. The homes are identical inside and out and built adjacent to each other.

They also constructed a new security building and gate at the entrance to the farm, where they re-hung the old metal "Finca El Milagro" sign. Only this time, the sign was restored to its original glory.

The homes are large ranch-style buildings with exteriors painted a warm yellow and topped with terracotta roof tiles.

Each has a covered porch with cushioned chairs and, like most houses in El Salvador, metal bars lining the windows. Dark wooden doors invite you inside.

I hesitated before Gary and I walked inside the girls' home, which they named the "Hope" home. Each time I had visited previously, our team was asked to remove our shoes to help keep the house clean. This time, I was assured it was okay to leave them on.

As we entered, I was reminded how comfortable the house was. It had an open-concept floor plan with high ceilings and was showered in natural light. There were modern fixtures and appliances, and cheerful, decorative accents.

Juan Carlos, the resident houseparent, greeted us. He was a big, tall man with a gentle disposition. His wife, Milagro, wasn't there yet. But we decided to start the interview while we waited. Gary once again translated.

I asked Juan Carlos to share how he ended up working at La Casa.

"In 2008 I was working as a bank manager," he said. "They only gave me one day off. My prayer was that God would give me a place where I could serve, but also be with my family. And I started looking in the newspapers and saw this announcement for foster parents. So I sent in my resume."

It was normal in El Salvador for employers to process CVs slowly. Sometimes it would take a month or longer. To his surprise, La Casa called him immediately to schedule an interview. But they required that both Juan Carlos and Milagro be present.

"I said to Milagro," he continued, "'Come with me. I have something that might interest you.'"

They went to La Casa and first spoke with the director.

"I felt from the moment I walked in, this is where God was saying, *I want you to serve.* And once we finished, the director said, 'I know that it's God calling you here.'"

Gary chuckled and interjected his own thought. "Now, you have to understand that Milagro doesn't know what's going on."

I had heard this part of the story years before, but it was like hearing it for the first time.

"Ooooh, she doesn't know it's an interview for a *job*," I said.

"No." Juan Carlos shook his head and let out a boisterous laugh. It was contagious.

Then they interviewed with several other people, including Gerardo and Sandra, the houseparents at the time.

"Gerardo's sister graduated with me from high school," Juan Carlos said. "Sandra was the sister of a friend. I felt an instant connection to them. We had a lot in common – we loved working with children, playing basketball. Gerardo said, 'You need to talk to Gary.' And Milagro says, 'Juan Carlos, what's going on?'"

His laugh was more forceful this time, making us all laugh harder.

"Before we went into the interview with Gary, I told her, 'It's more or less like being foster parents – it requires both of us.'"

Right then, Milagro entered the room and said, "Hola!" in a high-pitched, singsong way. She gave us hugs and sat with us. She was petite with medium-brown long hair.

Gary picked up the story. "When I interviewed them, I had no idea she didn't really understand what was going on," he said. "But I knew, the Holy Spirit was clearly speaking...and tears were falling because we felt the Spirit moving in all of us. There was no doubt."

Milagro began to share her side of the story. She spoke with a quick, confident cadence.

"Juan Carlos didn't tell me what this was about. He said, 'I've sent in my resume to work to be a dad. But you have to come with me.' As we entered the front door, he told me, 'I'm going to work here.' Jennifer came out and grabbed Juan Carlos's hand right away. She was eight years old. So Jennifer was the one that took us to begin the interview process. And then she looked up and said, 'Are you going to stay here with us?'"

The director "automatically assumed that I knew it was for the two of us," Milagro continued as Juan Carlos quietly laughed. "I said, 'I'm sorry, I'm just coming along with Juan Carlos.' I quit working when I was pregnant with Sofía. My day was already planned out, and it didn't have anything to do with working outside the home. So I said, 'I can't do that. Who's going to stay with the kids?'" They had two young daughters – Sofía and Elena. Their son, Marcos, would be born several years later.

"Every time [the director] would get up to bring somebody else to sit down and interview, Juan Carlos would reiterate, 'I'm going to work here.' He said, 'But don't worry, this process takes a while, we'll have time to see if this is right or not.'"

But it *didn't* take a while.

"We had one interview after another, without even getting much time in between. One of the things that gave us assurance, was at the end of each interview, they would say, 'The idea is not for you to just drop your kids and do this.' Because that was my only question. I wasn't looking for work." She laughed.

"After we went back home, we continued to talk and Juan Carlos kept saying, 'I'm sure this is it, this is what we're supposed to do.' So, I gave in." Milagro shrugged her shoulders. "I saw the passion in him – I just had to be with my husband in this."

In the beginning of working at La Casa, some days were good, others not so much. After a month, Milagro started to question if she belonged there. Some of the girls hadn't accepted her and would insult and mistreat her.

"Whenever I'd start thinking this isn't my calling, the Lord would confirm this is for me. God would show me the way to maneuver through those moments one day at a time. I began to love the children, love what we were doing, and love the place where we were working. It grew over time. One girl didn't talk to me for a year and a half. But then our relationship became very close. Then I began to understand God's purpose for having us here. I understood that one of the principal purposes that God had me in this place was not necessarily what I was going to do in the children's lives, but what He was going to do inside of me.

"Before, I was very much focused on my own family – my husband, children, sister, mother, our family. But God opened my heart for eighteen more young girls. In time I began to feel a love for them just like my own children. When you look in my hair and see gray hairs, each one has a name on it." She laughed.

"God continued to work on me to understand how to work with each one, because they're all very different. Many times I've wanted to leave. Many times I've questioned, what am I doing. But the Lord hasn't left me and hasn't let me leave. God's been faithful to continue to provide that little something to keep me here. Now after ten years, if I were to leave, it would be like abandoning my own children. So I've asked the Lord for strength, to refresh the way I see things, and to just take it one day at a time."

That led to my next question.

"What does a typical day's routine look like?" I asked.

"Juan Carlos gets up between 4 and 4:30 a.m., same as the girls. He comes in and makes breakfast and everybody has their own chores and things they have to do in the morning. I get up a little later and prepare their snacks and things they have to take along with them for school. Once everything is ready, we go separate ways. Juan Carlos goes with some of the kids to their schools, and I take our own kids to their schools. And sometimes we switch.

"Once we drop the kids off at school, we'll go by the supermarket and pick up something they need for lunch, or to a meeting. But now that Alicia has come into our lives, we're with her every morning." Alicia was a young girl with Down syndrome who had recently joined La Casa.

"The girls start arriving here from school between one and one thirty p.m. Once they've finished their lunch, then it's time to start doing homework. Generally I'm the one preparing the lunch and Regina helps me put that together. Either Juan Carlos or I will hang back and help the kids with homework, along with Tia Silvia, and the other one will go out and pick up our children from school. Some of the older ones get out at 3 p.m. So we have different hours of returning home. Then about 6 p.m. we start working on dinner."

"Does everybody work on dinner together?" I asked.

"No," she said. "A lot of homework is given – hours of homework. That's pretty common. In high school is when they have the most homework. They come home and after lunch they start doing homework until dinner and beyond. So, either I, or sometimes Silvia helps me, or Juan Carlos, will start getting dinner together. About a year before they leave to go to the transition house, we'll start incorporating them into preparing dinner, especially if we see they have a few minutes. Then they'll just jump in."

"On Fridays, typically, when homework doesn't have to go late they will sit down and do devotionals together after dinner. Usually by 10 p.m. everybody's in the bed. I wish they could go to bed earlier, but we can never seem to get them into bed that early. These girls are up talking, doing their hair, or something like that."

"Typical girls," I said.

"Yes, and the next day it starts all over again."

"Can you think of some of the positive changes you've seen in the girls since they started living with you?" I asked.

"One of the positive changes we've seen is that the girls feel more sure of themselves. They have more of a sense of belonging. They don't feel like outcasts anymore, especially in school, because they're part of a family. They're feeling less like victims."

"How often do the girls get to visit with their biological families?"

"Their biological families come here once a month."

"Have you seen those relationships grow over the years?"

"Yes, I've seen those relationships growing closer."

The conversation turned toward one family in particular, where five sisters were currently living at La Casa.

"These girls have learned to appreciate and love their mother despite her defects. They've accepted her as mom. Now they sit and really talk with her, where before they didn't have a great relationship with her. Sometimes [their mom] doesn't give the best advice, and now they're saying, 'Mom, I don't think that's the best thing to do.'"

There was another set of sisters in whom Milagro had seen similar changes.

"They're more aware of their mom's needs and they're concerned about their mom, where before it wasn't that way," she said.

"I understand my role," is to "represent their mom, in [her] absence. Because they have the example of a mom – I'm here to help them understand a little more – it's helped their relationship when their mom does come here. I can encourage them, 'Go share this with your mom, go tell your mom this, how about doing this.' It's been a way to help bridge that gap. When we seem them and their mom come in, it helps me feel this is what it's all about, this is what we've been working toward."

"So I'm still learning and working to try and help them understand what a mother's role is. They're not always crazy about it. Sometimes yes is yes and no is no. They don't always understand. But I think they're learning over time, this is the way it's supposed to be."

"We live like a normal family would, except as an extended

family. Sometimes we go out and suddenly we'll meet some of our friends that we've been friends with for a long time. And they'll say" – Milagro's voice hushed to a whisper – "'Are *all* of those yours?'" She laughed. "Yes, they're mine."

Chapter 10

Grace

ROSA ELENA MET US AT HER FRONT DOOR with a warm smile and hug. As I greeted her in English, I knew she understood me well, though she didn't speak much English. Her eyes were soft and welcoming.

Gary and I were invited to the boys' home, also called the "Grace" home, for lunch. Metaphorically speaking, the Grace home had ties to a small treehouse that sat above the pavilion, just up the hill from the house. A man had been invited by a family member to help build the treehouse and after only a few visits to La Casa, caught their vision to care for the children in El Salvador.

When La Casa entered a season of fasting and praying to hear from God concerning the building of the home, the man caught wind of their need for funding. So, he and his family's business provided the funds. While I didn't speak to this man directly, I was told he also has a ministry in Richmond, Virginia, helping move people out of homelessness and into independence. He's a humble, behind-the-scenes guy, I was told, who probably wouldn't want his name shared in this book.

The smell of food simmering in the kitchen was invigorating. As we waited, seven-year-old Samuel snuggled up to Gary and gave him a long hug – with eyes closed and a smile that stretched across his face. It was obvious how much Samuel craved that hug, especially given the physical and emotional trauma he had recently experienced. A large scar ran from his lower jaw down to his neck.

For a few minutes I played on the floor with Samuel's little brother. He had experienced the same trauma as Samuel but wore visible proof on his ear, instead. He had a little cough but was perfectly content to stack and restack Legos, laughing when they towered too high and fell down as if it were a game of Jenga.

There were seven boys living in the Grace home. When the food was ready, we all sat down together at a large square dining table – Rosa Elena with her husband (Ceferino), the seven boys, Gary, and me. We were treated to a meal typically eaten at Thanksgiving, our plates filled with salad, a pork, rice, and cheese dish, and a red hibiscus tea drink.

As we ate I was struck by the strong sense of family. One of the newest boys living in the home called Rosa Elena *mamá*. Another lifted his empty plate to show Rosa Elena, proud of his accomplishment of eating all his food. Samuel scowled when he bit into a green olive for the first time, and giggles erupted across the table. He paused for a moment, his head slightly tilted down as he eyeballed the other boys from above his eyeglasses, and cracked up.

The next day we went back to the boys' home to interview Rosa Elena and Ceferino about their experiences at La Casa. The boys were away at school.

Rosa Elena wore white pants and a black short-sleeved blouse, her dark silky hair draped to the middle of her back. Ceferino was standing at the kitchen island talking with Hilda. He peeled mangos while she chopped tomatoes in preparation for lunch.

Gary, Rosa Elena, and I sat down in the seating area on dark leather chairs. A few minutes later, Ceferino walked over and sat down beside Rosa Elena. He wore a white button-down short-sleeved shirt, blue jeans, and loafers. His demeanor seemed serious. Gary prepared to translate for me.

Right before Ceferino and Rosa Elena joined La Casa, she worked selling real estate and he was a pastor. They were often surrounded by others, including their immediate and extended families, and their church community. Ceferino participated in children's camps during the holidays. But amid the activity, spending quality time with their son and daughter, Daniel and Milena, was a priority.

"What brought you to La Casa?" I asked.

"Sandra invited me to go down," Rosa Elena said. This was in 2005, when La Casa was located at the city center in San Miguelito.

"We were actually their pastors," Ceferino said about Gerardo and Sandra. "We were encouraging them to become a part of La Casa, without ever realizing that this would turn around and he would pull me back into the ministry," he laughed.

"I offered my services to cut hair for the children," Rosa Elena said. She was also a cosmetologist. "I was impacted by the number of small children." Ceferino and Rosa Elena would also help take the kids to church camp. They continued serving with La Casa for two years, building relationships with the children over time.

Through their consistent involvement with the ministry, La Casa recognized that Ceferino and Rosa Elena would be a good fit for the role of houseparents. So, in 2007, they were interviewed for that position. But there was a delay in finalizing the offer and Ceferino was given another opportunity to pastor a church. So, he took the pastorate instead.

"I think that was just part of God's timing," he said. "Our biological children were small at that point. They required a lot more time and care from us. But we still were feeling called to be a part of La Casa."

"I still continued to cut hair and be a part of the children's lives," Rosa Elena said. "I used to take French bread in, and the kids were always happy because I was bringing a snack or something for them to have."

"In 2011 Ceferino received an invitation to pastor a church in Maryland. So he put in his resignation to the church here in El Salvador," she continued. "We had one foot on the plane, making preparations for the move to the United States. Then one evening I entered into the online page for immigration – it said that the process had been stopped because the church hadn't followed through on some of their responsibilities in Maryland."

"Without knowing it, this was the moment when Gerardo contacted us saying, could you cover us for a while," Ceferino added.

Gary quit translating and switched to English. "Let me explain. I'll give you the other point of view," he said.

"At this point, Sandra and Gerardo had been with us seven years. They had been serving with us day in and day out with the children and they were absolutely fried. They needed a break. So we said to them, I think it's good that you would take a leave of absence, that you would get some rest. Then at the end of this, let us know where you stand."

That's when Gerardo suggested that Ceferino and Rosa Elena cover for them. The timing was perfect and the kids already knew them.

Rosa Elena continued, "About two weeks in, after we had been covering for Gerardo and Sandra, they invited us to come out to eat. We said, 'Don't worry, things are going well. We've continued purchasing the same foods that you have, so that when you return things will be just as if you were here.' But they said, 'Feel free to make any changes, because we don't feel called to continue. We doubt we'll come back.'" So we said, 'Okay. We're going to continue covering for you because that decision is not our decision to make. It's God's and Gary and Sharon's decision, at the end, would we be houseparents or not.' It was Christmas time. We took the kids to our house to celebrate Christmas and it went well."

"For us it was a special time because God was confirming that now was the time for us to be a part of La Casa," Ceferino said. "One of the things I liked is Gary said to me, 'No day is ever alike in La Casa.' And it's been that way ever since." Ceferino laughed as he mused at the thought. "There are no two days alike, ever. It's not monotonous or boring." A short pause. "It's a little stressful at times," he added as the air in his voice escaped and his laugh turned into a belly laugh.

"January 2013 was the moment we were approached by Gary and Sharon, offering us to continue being houseparents," Rosa Elena said. Before they accepted, the entire family had to be on board. "We had a chat with our (biological) kids, to ask if they were in agreement with that decision."

"When we announced to the children at La Casa, that we were going to come on, some of the kids were excited. Then on the other side, there were some that all of a sudden, their attitudes changed." Rosa Elena grew quiet as tears rose to the surface.

"It's been a beautiful journey and there have been lots of moments we've really enjoyed. It's been hard. Some of the things that have made me sad, are wanting to dig in and help the different people that have been a part of our lives through this." There was a break in her voice.

"One of the boys we had even wanted to adopt (out). We received the news that the adoption was not going to go through."

Her voice was rich with emotion. "Ceferino took him to the bathroom and the little boy said, 'Why does this always happen to me? Every time I felt like I was going to be part of a family, I get shot down and it doesn't happen.' But we were able to, in time, see him get beyond that rejection, that moment. This was one of the more difficult times I've had at La Casa."

Rosa Elena quietly prompted Ceferino.

"Once I remember that Gary and Sharon challenged us to love these kids like they were our own," Ceferino said. He choked back emotion as his own tears fell. "I think that was the biggest challenge we had ever received. I can say that we consider these kids as our own. We cry with them, laugh with them. My life will never be the same having been here."

"I'm still a pastor and I share with the congregation that this ministry helps me be more understanding, more human. I've exchanged those moments when I wore a shirt and tie and coat, for times when we go pick mangos. Or wash cars with them. Or put shoes back there." He gestured over his shoulder and laughed. "For taking them to school, for washing dishes." The mood was light again.

Rosa Elena laughed at a new thought. "Sometimes when they come back from a soccer game," she said, her voice turning dramatic, "they'll say, 'Ceferino, can you please give me a massage right here?'" She pointed to her foot.

There was a long pause.

"I've learned as part of this ministry, that I need to have my own heart healed. Instead of coming to help, I've come to be helped," Ceferino said. "My patience has been tested in all ways. Especially in the mornings when the boys have to be awakened to get up."

"One of the things is to be a part of the battle, to be part of the fight to watch them as they begin to accept Jesus, accept what God wants for them. We're convinced that God's Word does the transformation. We continue to work in that, to see a complete transformation in their lives."

"We believe strongly that He who has begun a work in us, will see it through to completion," Rosa Elena added.

That seemed like a good segue for my next question.

"Is there a memory you'd like to share about one of the boys, maybe one of the things you've seen change in him since he's been with you?" I asked.

"Esteban was a kid with a lot of emotional issues," Ceferino said. "He was probably the one we had to deal with the most. Everybody knew that if something happened in the house you could look to Esteban as the one that did it. If something was lost, it was Esteban. If something was broken, it was Esteban. We would often call out Esteban's name when he wasn't even the one that did it," he said with a smile.

"I'll never forget that just before he left to go to the States." Ceferino choked up again and paused for a long moment. "The hug that he gave me. He said, 'Thank you for everything. I promise you, that I'm going to do well and I'll behave myself with the new family.' Those words were the most impactful. The family sends us photographs and he seems so happy."

It's not as common for children to be adopted out of El Salvador, as it is for neighboring countries. It isn't highly promoted in-country, either. Adoption court cases are long and drawn out, sometimes lasting three to five years, making it difficult for older children to be adopted before they turn eighteen. La Casa also strives to reunite their kids with family members before adoption is considered. In Esteban's case, he only had a mother who was unable to care for him for medical reasons, and he was placed on the adoption list at an early age.

"He has a great deal of intelligence that will help him in life. We, without knowing, put Esteban into a bilingual school, years before the adoption was even mentioned. This was always part of our prayers for him, that God has great plans for Esteban. I don't doubt that he will be a great man."

"And Mario," Rosa Elena added. "When he came in with his sister, Ana, in the beginning they were full of lice. I remember that Sandra called me over to come and cut their hair. So we threw this white piece of plastic trash bag down in the back yard, and I began to cut both of their hair."

"He had these big puffy cheeks and an extended stomach. He hadn't eaten well, and he was full of parasites. Mario and Ana had never been to school. Even with that beginning, right now he's in his first year of high school."

"He was one of these kids that was filthy dirty. He would play and sweat and run through the dirt. Never wearing shoes. If you said, 'Come on, Mario, we need to do something,' he would lay down on the ground and reach back and say, 'Wait a minute, I'm tired.'" Rosa Elena feigned drama in her voice and laughed.

While I didn't know Mario back then, I knew he had changed. When teams visited La Casa and toured through the boy's home, Gary enjoyed showing Mario's closet. It was organized and color-coordinated, everything in its proper place.

"Even to hear his reasoning now," Rosa Elena continued, "that he's someone that still makes mistakes, but he always understands and comes to the conclusion of, 'Here's where I messed up.' He'll go back and reflect on those things."

Life change was a major theme that presented itself as I spoke with people at La Casa. But not just in the lives of the children.

"What is the biggest thing that has changed in your hearts since being houseparents at La Casa?" I asked.

Ceferino answered first. "In our Latin American culture, what we call machismo, without even being aware of it, I was brought up in a home that was very *machista*."

From *Machismo and Matriarchy* by José L. González, machismo "assumes man's self-evident superiority to woman. He has the right to rule over her because she belongs to him and exists for his benefit, to serve his needs and desires."[12]

"I thought it was a normal way to treat my wife, because I saw my father treat my mother that way. As a pastor I thought I wasn't affected by that. I had to ask for forgiveness for my way of acting. I understood that I wasn't being a good example for my children. There began a change in the way I was thinking. In my way of treating my wife, in my way of working at home. I'm still in that process. I think it's going to be an eternity. I would have never discovered this. Like a cancer that was invading my being without me even noticing it. And God had to come in and cut it out directly, face-to-face."

There was another long, quiet pause as the weight of his words settled. I admired his vulnerability in sharing his personal struggle.

Rosa Elena answered next, her sentences formed slowly at first.

"When I was a little girl, I used to close my eyes and say, 'I want to have a big family.'" She smiled, her words tender with a catch in her throat. "But, for me to have the ability to love so many people. But I was dreaming as if it was me that was going to love all of these people alone – it was all for me. After marrying and having children, God has made this dream come true. Honestly, I never realized that my own family could also be a part of loving these children, too."

She picked up a framed photo from the table and handed it to me. There was giddiness in her voice as she described it. Twenty-two people were huddled together, arm in arm, with a white fluffy dog. It was a family photo with Ceferino and Rosa Elena standing with Milena and Daniel, members of Rosa Elena's family, the La Casa boys and young men from the transition home. It was Mother's Day.

"When I see my siblings and parents love these children the

way we do, I see God working through it all," she said.

Our time was nearing an end.

"Is there anything else that you'd like to share?" I asked.

"When I wake up at 4:30 in the morning, I drink a cup of coffee, go outside, and ask God's blessing," Ceferino said, growing emotional again. "My faith has grown a lot. Even coming through the [La Casa] entrance can be dangerous, every day. When my kids are getting out of school and I have to go pick them up, it's nighttime. I start saying Psalm 23." We all laughed for a moment. "I've never felt God's presence so strong. And the protection. We sleep peacefully. Inside this place is paradise. But what's around us is unbelievable. I also know there are a lot of people praying for us. We're thankful to God, to be a part of this big story."

Chapter 11

Breaking and Revealing

SOMEWHERE IN THE DISTANCE a man droned through a loudspeaker. He was far enough away that we couldn't see him. "La papa, la papa, la papa," he chanted like an auctioneer, over and over, his words strung together so quickly that I couldn't make them out without Sharon's help. His voice echoing through the streets was a daily occurrence, as he drove his truck and announced his fruits and vegetables for sale.

Sharon and I sat at the family table, with warm sunlight filtering through the large window beside us. The table doubled as Sharon's desk for computer and paperwork. Writing La Casa de mi Padre's newsletter was on her task list for the week.

Sharon had a quiet confidence about her. She was the mom of six grown children and had overseen La Casa for more than sixteen years. She was organized and an implementor of ideas.

"We've learned a lot along the process," Sharon said, referring to how the structure of La Casa had changed over the years. "We really believed that children would do best in families. But when we met this group of [fifty-nine][13] children downtown...and we had no money." She shook her head from side to side.

Moving the children from the abandoned warehouse into a large group home was only a step in the right direction.

"We just knew it wasn't what it was supposed to be, but we didn't know what else to do. But God always pushes in the right time and the right way," she said, hinting at the lessons learned through Diana and Marina's adoption.

By 2006, La Casa had teenagers under its roof and it became vital to separate the boys from the girls. That meant moving houses again and finding a couple who would care for the boys, and another for the girls.

"The concept was homes that run as foster homes. The mom and dad in that home, they have enough training and we have enough confidence in them, that they run the home. We shouldn't be in the day-to-day. But we should be the support around them to keep them healthy."

The new model allowed up to eight children in each home, plus the houseparents' biological family.

"La Casa would assume the role of raising funds. Many people have asked us, 'Why don't your houseparents work and provide for their home?' But we don't see how they can do that. We want the parents transporting the kids. We want them cooking and having meals together. We want them functioning as a family, so they've got to be there."

"So each family has a weekly budget. They choose how to use that budget, as a family...to model that for the children. Because they've come from families with such brokenness, that they've not been able to experience what a healthy family is. Our desire is that they would desire…a family in the future, to break those cycles."

There was one more area in which the houseparents were financially supported.

"Just if you had that many kids in your home, the family needs breathing room, too. They need some time to just get away."

With so many children in each home, there was extra help for the parents as well. Each home had a *tía* or *tío* ("aunt" or "uncle"). They assisted with homework when one-too-many children for the houseparents to answer, raised their hands. And if someone needed to burn extra energy, they might plan recreational activities for the afternoon.

The *tía* and *tío* worked for La Casa 40 hours each week. A typical schedule was Monday – Friday, with the houseparents given the freedom to set their hours however desired. The boys' home had two women who rotated in and out, so they could give the boy with autism the one-on-one attention he required.

La Casa was aware, from early on, that they wouldn't be able to properly care for that boy into adulthood. So as he grew closer to aging out of La Casa, they petitioned the courts to see if there was another home in the area that would be able to better care for him long-term. After a long, difficult court case, in 2020 he was transferred to a special needs home in San Salvador and was thriving. He had been with La Casa since he was a baby, so his transfer left a hole in the hearts of the La Casa family.

"Then we have the psychologist because our kids come to us with pasts that they need to sort out and work through, because you don't want them to carry that on, you want freedom from that," Sharon said.

Finding a psychologist who was a good match for the children had been a struggle in the past. Multiple psychologists came and went, which was detrimental to building the children's trust, a vital component for them to openly share their thoughts and feelings. But, finally, La Casa found the right person.

"Our psychologist's responsibility is to work individually with the kids when they need it. For some of our kids who have been with us for years, they don't need a session every week. They're beyond that. But she also does group sessions in each home to talk about living together, getting along...someone coming in, how do we treat a new person," Sharon said.

Once a child reaches fourteen years old, they begin to discuss life planning topics like the child's personal interests and career aspirations. The psychologist is also responsible for working with the biological family members of the children. She builds the agenda for staff training, too.

Sharon admitted having a single counselor wasn't sufficient to handle both the children's and transition homes. "We need to bring in another one, and possibly a third one. She has a huge responsibility right now."

Another key role in La Casa's organization is played by social workers, who are "really, partly legal," Sharon said. "They work with the courts or when there's referrals, and they get all the paperwork together. Most of our kids come without birth certificates, which means they come without an identity in the country."

When a birth certificate was missing, the social workers were the ones who slid down the bunny hole to secure one. In order for the child to have a birth certificate, the mother had to have one, which meant her mother had to have one. Often the social workers started with the grandmother, if she could be found, to eventually get a birth certificate for the child.

"Their goal is to try and find out if there are biological family members connected with the child to assess whether it's a healthy relationship or what was the root cause of separation." La Casa usually received some information from the courts, but it wasn't always comprehensive. "So they do a lot of digging in the community, with neighbors, and with the family, and try to create an intervention plan. What needs to happen in order for you to get your feet on the ground and to begin a healthy relationship, to reconnect and possibly reunify with your child."

It was the painful adoption of Diana and Marina that led La Casa to hire their first social worker. If they were unaware of the two girls' aunt and uncle, who had been looking for the girls, then which other children under their roof had family members they didn't know about?

"We started to look in all the cases," Sharon said. "Who else has family that maybe they shouldn't be with us. We tried to figure out, is there a real reason? And then no one's working with the family..."

I heard passion revving in Sharon's voice.

"Then all of a sudden a judge may say, 'Oh, two years is up, go back.' And if you've done nothing with that family, they go back to the same patterns. So it's trying to help. If it was addiction, whatever it was – sometimes it's multiple layers – what is the root cause, that's created all of this mess."

The children's cases were reviewed by the judge every three months. The social workers were responsible for documenting and compiling the necessary information, like developments within the child's family and in their stay with La Casa.

"Often before a case is seen, the judge has ten to fifteen minutes where she's reading everything and she makes a decision," Sharon said, "so making sure that those reports say what they need to say."

Three young siblings had recently moved into La Casa de mi Padre – a girl and two boys. Their mother was shot and killed at home, in front of their eyes, in a gang-related incident. One boy suffered bullet wounds to his jaw, the other to his ear.

It was sensitive cases like these that the courts, overwhelmed with the volume of cases, decided on in a matter of minutes. Sometimes that resulted in conflicting recommendations. In this case, the courts wanted to place the siblings back with a specific family member that loved the children. But she also lived close to where the shooting took place. La Casa was told the children couldn't live in that community again for their personal safety, especially since they were witnesses to the shooting and could become targets themselves.

The social workers made at least two family visits each week. With the number of families involved, that meant being in a specific family's home approximately once every six weeks. During the visit they discussed the plan for the child currently living at La Casa, assessed what was happening within the family, identified struggles, and determined any connections La Casa could help them make.

"We're not there to do it for them, but help them think through or find the resources that they need to get the help," Sharon said.

Many of the family members didn't know how to write their names. In situations where a signature was required, they had to use their thumbprint instead. So literacy classes were one of the resources La Casa helped them find within the community.

Once a month the social workers invited all the family members to the farm, where they engaged in planned activities for five to six hours. The goal was to create new memories for the families to build on. La Casa would provide conversation starters, and they might play games or hold races. The children would share their school report cards with them. La Casa also provided "Parent School," where they educated the families on parenting, communication, and discipline. The families would eat a light lunch, with everyone working together to serve the meal and clean up afterward.

Then the psychologist met with each individual family group to discuss specific concerns. For example, their child may have been expelled from school.

"If we can, when that happens we'll go get the family member, if there's a close enough relationship, and take them to school with us. Because we want to model, what do you do, how do you handle this?" Sharon said.

"Are there family bonds [with the La Casa children] that weren't there before?" I asked.

"I do think that the families we've worked with for a long time, I see a real connection where there wasn't before. Just the smiles and hugs of seeing each other," Sharon said. "Instead of us just handing them all the information, they begin to ask, 'Did you get a report card? Did you...?' They're learning how to communicate."

La Casa also wanted to teach the children how to be responsible members of their families.

"One of the hard cycles to break is that the kids couldn't wait for their mom or dad or aunt or uncle or grandma to come to bring them some Cheetos and a Coke. Like, you owe that to me," Sharon said. "And to help our kids process how can you serve your mom and dad. What's your role in this? What's your responsibility?"

Some of the young adults who lived at the Bridge couldn't, or chose not to, go back to live with their families because of the circumstances there. But La Casa encouraged them to go home and visit, especially during vacations.

"You don't go home empty-handed, expected to be fed and all, you're out in the real world. You take some food to share and you help cook, you babysit. Teaching them...because our kids have the tendency to just want to go back, okay, take care of me like a child because you never did."

One of the children that previously lived at La Casa was abandoned by his mother at the local dump. She lived at the dump, earning money by reselling items collected from the trash. Other organizations became aware of her living situation and raised money to build a small cinder block home for her. When it was complete, they celebrated with a special ceremony and handed her the shiny key to her new house.

But she'd never used a key before.

After hours of practice, she was finally able to unlock the door on her own. Inside the kitchen was a new stove that they demonstrated how to use. But eventually she removed the burners from the top, placed them into the oven below, and converted the oven into a chicken roost.

Items she collected from the dump were piled inside the house and in the back yard. Her house attracted rats, including the oven and the bedroom mattress.

A short-term mission team that served with La Casa volunteered to help deep-clean the house. They eliminated the rat nests from the oven and bought a new mattress to replace the old one.

On the back porch the woman paced back and forth, pulling her hair. What she considered her pets, and the beautiful treasures stuffed in her old mattress – pictures she cut out from greeting cards tossed at the dump – had been taken away from her.

It was another lesson learned that good intentions can fall short.

La Casa partnered with several organizations in the United States that regularly sent mission teams to serve in El Salvador. Many teams spent a full week with La Casa. They'd spend time with the children and work on a specific project, for example laying bricks or repainting the inside of a home. There were also medical mission teams that provided general wellness checkups and dental care. It was common for La Casa to host twelve to fifteen mission teams a year.

"How do you help teams come in, in a way that's healthy [for everyone]?" I asked Sharon. There was a period of time when La Casa stopped hosting teams altogether.

"It's not healthy for the kids to see so many people come into their lives and just leave," Sharon said. "But we believe the experience of being here changes lives...that people stay engaged in the work having come and seen it. That's why we partner with *groups* of people, with churches, that our kids come to know as 'North Point' or 'Faith Bridge' or 'Dr. Knight.' People who continually come to visit. They see 'em as family. Different family members are coming [each time], but they have a connection point."

La Casa asked teams to send a team photo before their visit. The photo would get placed on the refrigerator inside each home. That helped the children become familiar with the faces that would be visiting. Likewise, La Casa sent names and photos of the children to the team ahead of time to help facilitate relationship building.

During the week, time with the children often included lunch together when they arrived home from school. Teams also had one or two scheduled play dates with the kids where they kicked a soccer ball and played other games, or made crafts. Aside from that, time together was intentionally limited. La Casa didn't want the children to have any confusion on who the authorities were in their life. The houseparents had the final say.

When teams gave their goodbyes after visiting, La Casa emphasized not making "I'll be back" promises. The children would cling to those words and be heartbroken when that specific person couldn't return. Instead, hearing that "North Point" or one of the other groups was returning reminded them that they weren't forgotten – they were loved.

Teams helped La Casa build relationships with their neighbors by visiting their homes, asking about their specific needs, and praying with them. That included bringing a gift just to show their care – a small bag filled with food staples like rice, beans, sugar, and oil. The community surrounding Finca El Milagro contained the most vulnerable – those with few resources to care for themselves and their families, including elderly widows. Sometimes team members shed tears, struck by the disparity of life between the United States and rural El Salvador.

After visiting the neighbors, teams gathered under the large pavilion, a short walk up the hill from the children's homes. It was framed by knobby tree trunks, capped with terracotta tiles, and contained rustic, picnic-style benches.

"What does it mean to live in poverty?" Gary would ask.

Teammates shared their answers out loud as they processed all they had seen and heard during the walk through the community. They commented that although the Salvadorans were poor in possessions, they were joyful. So Gary would challenge the team a little further – that poverty wasn't limited to material things. It was possible to be poor in spirit and relationships, too. *All* of us lived in poverty in our own way. It wasn't our responsibility to rescue anyone from poverty, either. It was our responsibility to show them they had value in God's eyes.

"How has your faith grown through working with La Casa?" I asked Sharon.

"It always brings me to tears when we go on the land," she said, "and you can see the homes and the pavilion and the chapel in the background...you can see the whole picture. It's a faith that God's going to bring the right people along to want to support, and how He's done that over and over."

"Gary," she continued, "he's a visionary – once he's dreamed it, he thinks it's done and he's off to the next dream. I'll be the one to sometimes say there's no way that can get done." Sharon laughed. "It's a continuous surrender to [God].

"I don't think it's about La Casa and the ministry so much as it's about God's individual people. All of us come, I think, into the project often as, what we have to offer and the good we're going to do. But it's the breaking and revealing and healing that takes place in our own hearts."

Chapter 12

Horse Healing

I SAT AT THE TABLE with Whitney at her parents' house. Sharon stood in the kitchen cooking dinner with Loli, the smell of chile relleno floating into the room. A *pop! pop!* sound pierced the air as Gary waved a tennis-racket-shaped gadget in front of him. A mosquito zapper.

Whitney resembles both Gary and Sharon with blue eyes, full lips, a large smile, and dirty blonde hair. Scars on her arm are the only visible evidence of the accident. She speaks with airy, high tones, the softness in her voice, inviting.

She was fourteen years old when they started visiting the children at Sonia's house. "I loved going to play with the kids and I never really saw the other side of it," she said. "God closed my eyes to it," referring to the dirt and grime. When La Casa opened, she spent her free time there on weekends and vacation days from school. "They had my heart."

When Whitney's senior year of high school arrived, she was

faced with the decision of where to attend college the next year. After forming strong bonds with the La Casa kids, saying good-bye would be difficult. For that reason, she wasn't sure she wanted to attend college in the States, but her parents encouraged her that she could get a degree that would enable her to work with the kids.

"And so, since I really liked science, I chose physical therapy because it was less time than a doctor in school." Whitney grinned and laughed quietly. "So I went to Bridgewater College. But after my first year I was like, okay, there has to be a way to combine my two passions."

Whitney had loved horses since she was a little girl. Her grandfather owned horses and the family would watch them compete in shows. She wasn't allowed to ride the horses but she could go to the barn and pet them.

When they moved to El Salvador, a friend invited her to take riding lessons for $5 an hour. So, with her parents' permission, she took her first lesson. And she never stopped riding. She rode horses all through high school during PE.

"I started researching and found the only university in the US that offered Therapeutic Horsemanship as a complete degree." So, Whitney moved out of Bridgewater and enrolled at St. Andrews University. Then the accident happened. She deferred enrollment until August of the following year and eventually earned her degree, in spite of the setback.

"My senior project was to come up with a business model and mine was to do a riding center here for the kids. It was my dream I thought I'd be getting to ten years down the road." Whitney recounted the first two weeks back in El Salvador after graduation. She had kept her dream quiet. "But people kept coming up to me and saying, 'When you're ready, I'll help you get some horses,' or 'When you're ready, I'll help you get things for your barn.' And so I told my dad, I think God's telling me I need to stay."

Whitney contacted the only other therapeutic riding center in El Salvador and paid them a visit. The main therapist asked her a few questions and then immediately put Whitney's skills to the test. Whitney had to give a boy his riding lesson that day. That experience led to Whitney volunteering for, and eventually working for, the center for the next year and a half.

"That was God laying the bricks. I met vets, people who sold hay, a farrier that shoes the horses. It was actually where my first two horses came from, from the program. They were their rejects. But I took them and spent a lot of time training them. People couldn't believe the changes in the horses and they were like, 'You're putting kids on these horses? No way! How?' I trained them. They just needed that care."

Whitney's dream came true when she formed her own Serenity Therapeutic Riding Center in Santo Tomás. At first it was only for the La Casa kids, who would ride once a month on Saturdays. Then she expanded it to include other children from the community.

Horses are used in therapy because of their unique ability to connect with their riders. "The horse has this extra sense," Whitney said. "They can not only feel what you're feeling, but they can mirror, or reflect, it back to you."

As the horse's behavior changes, Whitney receives a visual indication of how a child is feeling inside. "And so I always tell the kids, 'Talk to the horse. It's okay. He understands you. And he can't tell anybody your secrets.' Because I think the kids have such a trust issue with other humans, and knowing that they can trust the horse has helped them a lot." Being able to control a large animal gives them confidence, too.

Even caring for the horses has proved beneficial. "A lot of times, if I know a kid is quiet or just seems off, we won't ride and I'll have them groom the horse. Just that time spent brushing, the repetitive movements are so soothing. Sometimes you see them whispering or moving their lips and usually by the time they're done, they're in a much better mood."

Rodrigo was a twelve-year-old boy who lived in the community when Whitney first met him. He was a guest at La Casa's annual Christmas party for their neighbors. "He literally looked like he was sitting in a chair, that's how shrunken down he was. He had to hold onto his mom to walk. I just remember seeing him, thinking, if I could just get him on a horse."

At that time Whitney had only worked with the La Casa kids but had room in her schedule for more. "I walked up to him and said, 'Would you like to learn how to ride a horse?' And he looked up to his mom, asking her with his eyes, just begging. And she said, 'Well, how much does it cost?' And I said, 'No, it's free. I will not charge you.' Because I think that's been my thing is, if they can't afford it, it's okay because this is my ministry. This is what I'm doing to give back to God."

Whitney reflected on her first session with Rodrigo and how, after only his first ride, his torso was a little straighter. The warmth from the horse acted as a muscle relaxer, allowing the boy to stretch. He started to develop balance, too.

"Then I got him some hiking canes. Because where he lives it's mainly dirt. So he used those for a while. He's seventeen now. He comes every single Saturday to ride and he loves it. Now nobody helps him – he's up and down hills, stairs. He gets on and off the bus by himself. If you were to see him today, he is almost straight up and down."

Two years before my interview with Whitney, I watched her lead a riding session with several of the La Casa girls. The rectangular riding area sat near the base of the road that led up to the stable. Sometimes Whitney gave the horses free reign of the land and you had to be careful to jump out of their way when they trotted down the hill.

The girls sat straight up in their saddles as they commanded the horses. Whitney stood in a central spot where she kept a watchful eye on each rider and horse. They walked single-file around the ring.

Suddenly, one of the horses lurched forward like a rocket. The rider screamed in nervous delight as she labored to regain control of the animal. Whitney shouted instructions and soon they maneuvered back into place.

Another horse slowed and hovered near the back corner of the fence. Its rider had downcast eyes and pouty lips. This time, after Whitney's attempt to remedy the situation, the horse didn't move.

Whitney walked over to them and spoke quietly with her head tilted upward. The girl wiped her eyes with her arm. A slow head-shake. Then a nod. They huddled together for several minutes before breaking, Whitney's facial expression tender.

Pop! Pop! Another mosquito down.

The children form bonds with specific horses and sometimes a horse will behave differently depending on the person riding. Huracán, one of Whitney's white Arabian horses, had a special connection with one of the La Casa girls as well as Rodrigo.

"I've tried her on different horses and it just does not work. But she can get on Huracán and he will do anything she asks," Whitney said. "And how careful he steps when Rodrigo's riding him. You'll see the other horses in the ring are running around and going crazy, but he'll go slow and he makes sure that he's not going to trip."

Another La Casa child, a boy with autism, had a bond with Serena, one of Whitney's first horses.

"She had a wild personality, didn't mesh with most of the kids. But he would get on her and it would be a total change." Whitney snapped her fingers. "She'd be so calm and serene, like her name says, and just really careful."

The boy would approach Serena to bathe her, but often just sat underneath her belly, letting the water drip on him.

"The look on her face when he would be under there was, can I move? Should I move?" Whitney opened her eyes wide, her face frozen as she mimicked Serena. "She would stand so still until he got out from under her and then she would swat, go to bite a fly, or pick up her foot or something."

A few days later we visited the stable, nestled among the trees on La Casa's land. It stands up on a hill, accessible by a narrow, winding dirt road that you can easily miss if you don't know it's there. Her five horses – Corsario, Kiara, Luna, Huracán, and Kifa – were grazing in an adjacent field, swishing their tails at flying insects.

Whitney unlocked a small storage shed. Dark brown leather saddles and harnesses hung neatly on the walls. A few bags of horse feed anchored the floor. Shelves held brightly colored helmets, saddle pads, sand buckets, and shovels.

The barn was a covered, open-air unit with freshly poured cement foundation. The stalls were simple but effective: knee-high walls built from concrete bricks that supported wooden planks to fence in the horses. Sand covered with hay coated the floors.

Whitney was open about the financial challenges she's faced over the years.

"I started it on a huge leap of faith. I didn't have the money for any of it. It was like, okay God, if this is what you want me to do,

I'm going to do what I can. I don't know where the rest is coming from."

It had been eight years since she started the program.

"There have been maybe a day or two where the horses haven't had horse feed, or, lots of times where it's close to time to pay and I don't have the money and I don't know where it's coming from. You find ways to cut corners. I've become a pretty good vet, at least for the minor things." She laughed slyly. "But God has just been so faithful to provide. North Point actually, a couple of times now, has donated Be Rich money that has covered the cost for a year."

Be Rich[14] is a global movement of generosity started by North Point Ministries, with three main goals: to give, serve, and love. It was born from the charge presented to Timothy, to command Christ-followers who were rich, not to put their hope in uncertain wealth, but in God "who richly provides us with everything for our enjoyment. Command them to do good, to be rich in good deeds, and to be generous and willing to share."[15] Each year, North Point Ministries launches a Be Rich giving campaign and gives 100 percent of the money away – to partners making a significant impact in the world, including La Casa de mi Padre.

Financial challenges weren't Whitney's only ones.

"Last year a team rebuilt my barn. Over the years of replacing pieces of wood because the termites had eaten it, the stalls were falling down, literally. When they came to do that, I had been through a really rough time. I had lost my first horse, my favorite horse, and I was feeling like there was destruction all around me, and death. And I was just like, I don't know that I can keep doing this. The kids were not wanting to come ride and it was a fight."

"But the leaders had horses and they had built their own barn. And so, the words of encouragement they poured into me that week, and then to see the new barn done, how beautiful it was compared to the destruction beforehand. And the kids started to turn around, be a little more enthusiastic about coming to ride. It was like God saying, *Keep going, keep pursuing this. I have you here for a reason.*" She paused. "And I always tell him, 'Okay God, when you want me to move on from this and do something else, quit providing.'"

Warehouse where the children were first living, circa 2001.

Salvador (left) and Alejandro (right), circa 2002.
(Markings were on the paper photo, only.)
IMAGE RETOUCHED BY FRANCES BROWN

Daniela, 5 years old, on her second day of living at La Casa de mi Padre, May 2002.

The warehouse collapsed two weeks after the children moved out, June 2002.

Daniela (front) and Silvia (behind) riding bikes on the rooftop of the first La Casa home, circa 2005.

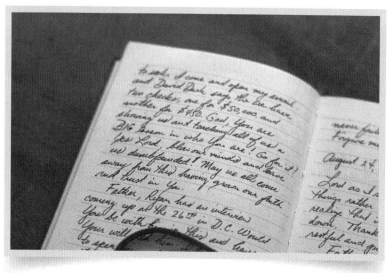

Gary's journal entry, August, 2005.

*Gary shares the plans for future land development at
Finca El Milagro, circa 2005-2006.*

Gary shares the plans for future land development at
Finca El Milagro, circa 2005-2006.

The chapel was the first building constructed
on the farm after it was purchased in 2005.

La Casa's home in Colonia San Francisco from 2006 - 2015.
© CHRISTINA STEWARD

A new soccer field at the farm, 2009. © GARY NIEBUR

Construction of the first two houses at Finca El Milagro, 2015.

The Grace and Hope homes were completed in 2015.

The security entrance to Finca El Milagro, constructed in the same style as the houses.

Salvador and his wife, Tia, with their son, Teo, 2022.
COURTESY OF SALVADOR AND TIA BARAHONA

Alejandro and his wife, Fernanda, standing inside the chapel, 2022. They had returned to the farm for their engagement photo session.

Silvia received her teaching certificate in 2017. In 2019, she completed her full education degree, becoming the first in her family to receive a university degree.

Whitney with her horse, Kiara, 2016.
© ADAM CAUDLE

*Frank and Whitney Magaña
during their engagement, 2017.*
© TATIANA LEAIR PHOTOGRAPHY

Daniela, 2021.

Gary and Sharon Powell, 2015.

Chapter 13

Working with Lives

SARAI HAD JUST RUN UP THE HILL from the children's homes to La Casa's office building, which sat on top of the highest point at the farm. She was breathing heavily with sweat glistening on her forehead. She had worked for La Casa for nine years in various roles, including administrative assistant and, most recently, in communications, where she helped with the sponsorship program and mission team logistics. She had shoulder-length curly hair and wore a peach-colored, long-sleeved T-shirt, dark blue jeans, and black Converse-style shoes. Sarai spoke English, so we didn't need a translator.

She described her early days working with the ministry.

"They interviewed with me saying...you will work with lives. You will work with these children who are so needy. I felt in my heart this is the place where God wanted me. So they said yes, and I started to work one week after that."

She recalled a moment when she was checking their inventory

of school supplies. "I was praying in my mind, saying, *Here's my life, use me.* And I heard clearly His voice telling me, *I didn't take you here to give to them. I took you here because I need to teach you.*"

Emotion rose to the surface of Sarai's face, and she grew quiet for a few seconds.

"Every day is so different. Here is not a common job. You don't have any normal days. Here you need to be so passionate about what you're doing, that any day isn't the same. And I love that." She paused. "I remember I used to give all the cleaning supplies to everybody, and we didn't have soap. I mean, the detergent?" She looked at me for approval of that last word.

I nodded.

"Okay. We used to buy one big bag every week and I didn't have anything, because we had to use more that week. I remember praying, saying, 'God, tomorrow, I have to give this to everybody. I don't have anything. What are we going to do?' A lady had just knocked on the door *that* day, saying, 'Hey, I have these bananas, I have these apples, and I have this detergent.'" Sarai smiled wide. "It was the *same* bag that I was needing." She clapped her hands together. "I remember running to the bathroom crying and praying, 'Thank you, God, thank you because you hear me.'"

She continued, "Also, I remember we used to write a check every week, one check for food. And we didn't have any money, maybe around sixty dollars. And we also had to pay the payroll, so we were like, 'What are we going to do?' I remember that we received something so we put that money into the account. But because of the payroll, it automatically covered all the payments, but we were still missing the money for food. Gary called me the next day saying, 'Hey, Sarai, there's some money in the account. Did you send something?' It was six hundred dollars. I said, 'No. I didn't receive anything.' So I called Peter, who's our accountant and he said, 'No, I didn't put anything.' Because sometimes the hotel used to give us a monthly donation...but no, we never knew where that money came from. So Gary told me, 'Maybe it's a mistake from the bank. We should wait, just in case they took back the money.' So we waited for two days and the money was still there. But it was exactly the amount we were needing to cover for it.

"Those kinds of testimonies I can tell you. But for me, La Casa de mi Padre, it's a place where you can do what God calls you to do, but also it's a place where He is training you. And until He's done in you, He won't take you. Yeah, sometimes the battles are coming one after another one and another one...so you feel like you are swimming on the sea, that a wave is coming when you're trying to catch a little breath. But after nine years I can tell you, this is a place where God's caring. This is not my fight. It's His. And He never loses any."

I loved the visual of a God who went to battle on our behalf and won – every time.

"Can you tell me more about the sponsorship program?" I asked.

"What we want to do is, any of us or any of the people who wants to share with La Casa can sponsor a child. And our specific needs are housing, transportation, health, clothing, some special gifts, all the things that we use to spend money at La Casa. If you choose one of the kids to sponsor, you can sponsor a specific need or a full sponsorship. So you are committed, not with La Casa, not with the children, you're committed with God. It's a partnership with them...knowing that this is for eternity. Because we're working with hearts, we're working with lives."

"Some people have given monthly, others have given annual, other people have given full sponsorship. But we have also really faithful people, that they are working with us, doing that. You know, everybody says you can do missions in three ways:

praying, giving, and going. And we are so thankful also for these people because they also are doing missions here in El Salvador with us, partnering with us, working with us. And sometimes they don't know the impact that they are doing with just five or ten or twenty-five dollars, that you can go and buy a T-shirt or maybe buy some food. But if you are just taking that money just to give for God, this has an eternal impact."

"Per policies, [the children] don't know who sponsors them," she added.

"They don't know? Because there could be multiple people that sponsor the same child?" I asked.

"Yes, right," Sarai said. "And sometimes, we don't have a children's sponsor yet. So they could think, maybe I'm not worth it that somebody would sponsor me. And that is not what we want."

"Also, we used to work with sharing, I mean, the sponsors can write the children, we translate the letters. And also the children, some of them write back. So we used to translate those letters and send them. And we used to work with four communications during the year, just to share, how are the kids doing. Talking about school, maybe a random topic. Talking about our Independence Day, and talking about a Christmas greeting saying thank you. That is what we used to do."

I noticed her "used to" phrasing. "So that's currently not—"

"It's currently," she answered before I could finish the question. "We're trying to work in something new."

"What's it like when teams come in?" I asked.

"I like the logistics. I like to organize that you are checked into the hotel, that you have water, the transportation is ready, they have the right schedule and everything."

The times I had visited La Casa with a team, the logistics and scheduling ran like a well-oiled machine. From our departure time from the hotel each morning to dinner in the evening, we never had to make decisions about where to be and at what time. We simply plugged in to the schedule given to us.

"It's nice to work with them," Sarai continued. "You know a lot of new people, their backgrounds, their stories. But also, sometimes for me, because sometimes I'm a perfectionist girl, when the schedule is not running as we said, I'm like, what are we going to do? So I'm always freaking out." She laughed. "But at the end, it's not about me. It's about what God wants to do. And sometimes I've seen that God used all those teams, to work in the lives of the team members. Even with us."

When I first met "Katy" Catherina in 2014, she toted a DSLR camera strapped to her shoulder. She was the communications coordinator for La Casa, of which one responsibility was to photograph the children in their day-to-day lives. The photos were used for progress updates sent to the government, as well as La Casa's newsletter and social media channels. I was immediately drawn to her gentle nature – she was quick to listen and slow to speak. She also spoke English, which allowed me to connect with her easily.

Now four years later, I sat across from her in a small but comfortable meeting room in La Casa's office building. She wore a white sleeveless blouse, light blue jeans rolled up at her ankles, and navy Toms-style slip-on shoes. Her long hair was pulled back in a ponytail.

I asked Katy to describe her role working with La Casa.

"I'm in charge of showing La Casa," she said, "to be like a window for people out of the country or even out of San Salvador to see that their time, their effort, their prayers are worthy – are getting results. Kind of being a filter between what's going on at La Casa and the world. So for me, it has always been a big responsibility. If you do something wrong, it's like a worldwide mistake. If it's a wrong [social media] post, or wrong picture, it's a wrong message. So you have to be very careful. I've learned to be very humble, to ask for help and guidance."

I could sense the weight of how seriously she took her role.

"I've learned to ask a lot of Sharon [Powell]," she continued. "Because two different cultures see things absolutely opposite. Something that is right here is not right there." Many of La Casa's supporters lived in the United States. "So, the first days I was scared to be here, I was like, I don't want to make a mistake. But the Powells trust us a lot. And that helps us to trust that we are close, that we are a family, a team. Even if I make a mistake, I trust that we can solve it together, and that's a big thing."

Katy was responsible for sending La Casa's emails, drafting newsletters, creating social media posts, and handling general communications, all of which aided in recruiting volunteers. She also forged connections with businesses that donated manufactured goods, which stretched La Casa's budget further.

"The kids," I said, "do you get to spend a lot of time with them? Do you see them every day?"

"I would love to see them every day," she said, "but there are days that I cannot. But, I look for opportunities to see them. I love them. They're part of our families, they're part of my family. My daughter loves them, knows them by name and age. She loves to share her stories and clothes and all that with the girls. My husband helps me every time he can."

It wasn't typical nine-to-five work.

"You pray for them, you get involved in their problems, you get worried for them, you receive phone calls or messages from them, like, 'I'm tired, I want to leave.' And I thank God for giving me that grace for them to share with me some things that have happened here."

"They feel safe coming to you," I said.

"Mmmm...hmmm." Katy nodded in agreement. "They trust. So for me that has been a gift from God. To share more than work, or more than taking pictures, to feel connected with them. I hurt when they hurt and I feel happy when they're happy. And you get invited to their graduation and you're proud to be there. To be working here is becoming part of a family."

"What do you think is one of the most challenging things about working here?" I asked.

"To do what God wants me to do. And I know that sounds spiritual, but no, it's not. It's like, being part of the process and not being an obstacle in their lives. You have the chance every day to say an encouraging word, or just to give a hug, or just to smile. And if you ignore that big blessing of being a blessing to these children, that's the big challenge. To try to avoid that important part of your work. This is *more* than work. So that's challenging because you have good days and you have bad days, grumpy days."

I laughed at the thought of Katy being grumpy. I had never seen that side of her.

"But you have to overcome those things. It's like being a parent. You have a lot of problems, but you have the opportunity. Because there are days when they're open and there are days when they're like, 'I don't want to talk.' So that opportunity when they open that door to talk, to say, 'My God, give me the words to say.'"

I admired her intentions to love the children well and how she sought God's guidance in the process.

"So, what's been the best part about being here in this role?" I asked.

"Being here, I've learned to understand the things I've lived in my life. There are times when you don't understand why things happen to you – I've been good, why did this or that happen to me. I've learned here that all of those things...are helping me to understand mercy, grace, restoration, healing, forgiveness. If [the children] ask me, 'Can I forgive my father for this?' yes, you can. And I can talk to them being sure that you can, because I've lived that. It's like God telling me, *I prepared you all those years before this moment. I've worked with you and, yes, you cried, and, yes, you suffered, and, yes, you lived all those things, because of this.* And that makes sense in my life. I understand why. I understand their pain. And I can cry with them and I can tell them, 'God loves you. What happened doesn't matter, you can be a professional and you can do whatever you want, you can achieve your dreams.' Sometimes they think they can't. Being at the other side of the bridge, you can tell them, you can."

"One of the beautiful things about getting older," I said, "is that you get this history with God. That you can look back and go, look at what He's done. It opens your eyes and deepens your faith, that...He's been working in your life all this time."

"Yes," Katy said, "you see things differently. I think that I trust God more than I did before. Because I've seen him working in my life, that makes me trust that He can do whatever He wants to do."

"Is there anything else that you'd like to share? Any specific memories?" I asked her.

"Well, something I'd like to share, something that really touched my heart and really helped me to do things right. One day I wanted to bring some volunteers for a party and it was Friday afternoon and [the children] were tired, and I was like, 'yeah, but they're volunteers and they want to come share with you. And one of the kids told me, 'They treat us like they're going to a zoo. We're not a zoo. We're not animals that they go and see and enjoy looking at."

I closed my eyes and grimaced at those words.

"That made me realize," Katy continued, "that sometimes

things that you think that you're doing right are not right. And you have to listen to them. They're the most important input you have to take. Because if you get used to, okay this is what I have to do, and you forget about their feelings...they have emotions and they're tired. But I really appreciated that [the child] was honest."

Katy told the child not to worry, to go and rest.

"So I learned, that they are the most precious thing that God has given us. And we are privileged to spend a while or a big part or a small part in their lives, because we don't know how long they're going to be here. So that tiny part in their lives I try to make it an unforgettable moment for them and for me."

Chapter 14

A Different Future

I SANK INTO THE SOFA across from Daniela. Gary squeezed in beside her and Sharon was at the kitchen table. Another young lady who lived at the transition home wandered into the kitchen to fix a snack.

Daniela was twenty-one years old. She wore a pink watch, an InsideOut[16] T-shirt with the shape of the State of Georgia on the front, blue jeans, purple socks, and Keds. Her straight long hair was thick and dark.

In Spanish, Gary explained to Daniela why I was there. Then, Sharon started to belly laugh.

"He joked that you were going to ask her different questions, like what color was the first pair of glasses she ever wore," Sharon said.

"Red," Daniela retorted with a smile.

Gary switched to English.

"You didn't pick those out, they were given to you. Do you

know who gave them to you?" he asked.

"So, Daniela understands English," I observed out loud.

"Yes, she does," Gary said. "But she won't speak it. At least to me. I think that if she had a boyfriend, maybe she would." He turned back to Daniela. "Do you have a boyfriend?"

"What?" she said with a giggle, pretending not to hear him.

"She's not going to answer that question," Sharon said, laughing.

"I'm satisfied with God, not boys, eternally," she said. More fits of laughter in the room.

"Okay," Gary said to no one in particular. His tone meant, *Let's get serious.* He was ready to translate for me.

I shifted in my seat.

"Do you have any memories of being at the house with Sonia?" I asked Daniela.

"Yes," she said. "I remember there weren't many rooms. There were some bunk beds. We had a trunk where the clothes were kept. But we would fight because the clothes weren't for a specific person, it was just a bundle of clothes. We ate very little. We had lice." She erupted with laughter at that last word, like an embarrassed teenager talking about having the cooties.

"I remember this group of North Americans came," she continued.

"To be nice," Gary interjected. "When we're not around, they call us 'gringos.'"

"They brought us boxes with many presents inside," she said. "For the girls they had little hair ties and mirrors." They were Christmas boxes distributed through Samaritan's Purse.

"How old were you?" I asked.

"Six. I cried a lot. I remember waiting in the doorway at night and it was raining, just waiting for my mother to come. I only remember the rainy days because we got wet. I remember Sonia saying, 'Don't worry, she'll come and get you,' but she never came."

As Daniela's thoughts trailed, Gary asked her another question and then translated it into English. "I asked if she remembered that first time we made her move," he said.

"When they moved us from Sonia's place over to the rented house," Daniela said, "I wondered, *What are we doing here?* They said, 'We're going to put these clothes on you, but these aren't your clothes.'"

"I remember you cut our hair," she continued, referring to Gary. "I remember taking a scrub bath and they took my hair and put that anti-lice shampoo in it. And they put some kind of white T-shirt on us. And shorts. That's when things changed. That's when we had our own clothes instead of just a community basket. We had nannies taking care of us, too. And there was one big long table where everybody ate."

"I remember one day we had to stay in our rooms, that we couldn't come out. So we were thinking, *What's happening?* Then everybody came out and we went upstairs (to the roof)."

Daniela smiled, and the pitch of her voice rose as excitement bubbled out.

"And they had put all this playground equipment up there for us. There were bicycles, there was a castle up there, there were swing sets. And we cut a ribbon for the new playground upstairs. That made us feel like it was ours. It changed our concept from where we had to share everything, to now something was for us."

"Did you have sisters with you?" I asked.

"No. That's another story," Daniela said.

"Sometimes I would feel bad about myself and in school they would tease me," she continued. "They would tease me about my glasses. I didn't like to wear them. And then I lost the glasses. I said, 'I don't need them.' Then we went to an ophthalmologist and the doctor said, 'Where's your glasses?' And I said, 'Oh, they broke.' The doctor said my problem was that I needed an operation. I got mad because they were always telling me I had to have the glasses on and in reality I didn't need the glasses, I needed an operation. But it was expensive."

"What was the operation for?" I asked.

"My right eye was facing in," she said. "I felt bad because the operation was expensive and I felt it would be a hardship for them (La Casa) to do it for me. Then later we moved to Colonia San Francisco. There was a staircase outside. I remember going up and sitting down on the staircase and saying to God, if He wanted to help me with the operation, that was fine. But if not, that was okay. And then we had a meeting out in the garden – some *other* North Americans came," she said with a laugh. "It was Bill Willits and Gary Niebur."

Gary interjected. "They presented us with our first Be Rich check."

"You cried," Daniela said to Gary. "And then you came to me and said, 'Daniela, we have the money for your operation.'"

Daniela grew silent for a few moments while she fought to control her emotions. Then she spoke with a catch in her throat. "God revealed to me how much he's into the details and smallest things in our life."

"So she did have her operation, shortly thereafter," Gary said. "And I can remember Daniela, looking at her for the first time, where she looked at me, and she was just beautiful."

Gary smiled at Daniela like a loving father.

"Daniela was one of the last people in La Casa that we had found family for," he said. "And a judge was about ready to sign [adoption] papers for her. And the judge says, 'I'm not signing these papers until we find Daniela's mother.'"

"I always had this desire to know who I was. My real name, details about myself, where I came from," Daniela said. "Catherine, the social worker, asked if I remembered anything about my family. I only remembered a name. Jonathan. And she said, 'Your mother?' No. I didn't remember anything about her."

"So, our social worker and counselor started to chase down leads that were coming out of the courts," Gary said.

They traveled to the eastern side of the country in search of Daniela's mother. They spoke with locals and asked questions, and even returned with photos of people with the same name as Daniela's mother.

However, none of the people in the photos looked like Daniela – not even a little bit.

"And so we prayed. 'Lord, we would love to find family for Daniela, but we don't know where to start. We don't know how to do it.' And after we prayed, I remember thinking and discussing amongst us, maybe we should call Sonia," Gary continued. It had been many years since they had spoken with her.

Sonia didn't remember much about Daniela's mother. But she did remember that she had a boyfriend who was a policeman.

When La Casa tracked him down, he gave them another lead – they might find her in a small town near the beach at Costa del Sol. So, they visited the town and stopped at the spot where everybody milled their corn. As they sleuthed, they received yet another lead that led them to a specific house. They knocked on the door.

"Weeks went by," Daniela said, after the social worker asked about her family memories, "then they called." La Casa had a surprise for her. "I went into their office and they showed me a photo album. They showed me family members that I didn't know. What I remembered was my brother, Jonathan."

"After that they took me to my family. I met everyone – my mother, brother, sister, my great grandmother, and great grandfather. And my nephew, uncles, aunts, and their children," she said. "And that's when we found out that my last name wasn't Flores." It was actually Romero.

"Oh...you didn't know before?" I asked.

"You didn't even know your birthday, right?" Gary asked her. "How old were you when this happened?"

"I think I was thirteen," Daniela said.

"So she went from six years old to the time when she was thirteen with no contact, no information, no anything," Gary said.

"Nothing," Daniela said, matter-of-factly. "Then began the process to reconnect us."

The Salvadoran judicial system insisted she be reintegrated with her family.

"I went home with my mother every two weeks. And living with her was really different. I didn't feel like her daughter," she explained. "The hardest part was my mom thought I didn't love her. Part of me was thinking, *She made the decision not to come back for me and raise me, but [for] my brother and sister, yes.* After talking with others, I cried. And I prayed. Ultimately I was able to forgive my mother. But I didn't want to live with her. I realized that God had not allowed me to live in that family because he had a different future for me. I wanted to study. I wanted to be a professional. If I had been with my family, that would not have been possible." There was a short pause. "I probably would've ended up pregnant."

Gary asked Daniela how her experiences have affected her faith in God.

"I've had moments in my life where I didn't believe in God. I felt abandoned. But these memories I have helped me to understand that He was always with me. Now I'm studying at the university and have two more years to go."

"What are you studying?" I asked.

"Psychology," she said. "I want to help children that have been through similar situations as I've gone through."

Chapter 15

Dream Coming True

"ALE" ALEJANDRO AND I SLID OUT CHAIRS as we sat under the portico at Union Church. His dark thick curls reminded me of my own. I met Ale a year and a half prior during a team visit to La Casa, when he was working as a *tío* for one of the homes. Many teams visited during the year, and it was difficult to remember every face, so I reminded him of our last exchange.

Ale reflected back on his time living at La Casa. He reminisced about another boy who lived there, who was a close friend until they had a falling-out. The other boy was passionate about Spiderman. But Ale's superhero was Batman. When it was the boy's birthday, La Casa threw a party and hung a Spiderman piñata. Ale promptly told the boy he was going to break the piñata on the first hit because he hated Spiderman. But when the birthday boy retorted that Ale wasn't going to hit his piñata at all, Ale stormed to his room while muttering the words "I hate you."

"At the beginning," Ale said, "it was all about play. But there was a point that I felt alone, even though I had my siblings there. I was always hiding in my room because I just did something wrong. That was the way I was showing my emotions – through anger."

Things turned for Ale when La Casa hired Gerardo as director, who eventually became a houseparent with his wife, Sandra. Gerardo took interest in Ale and asked him about the details of his day, even when Ale deserved discipline.

"We started going to Gerardo's church," Ale said. "When they introduced us...he was the first person who said, 'These are my new sons and daughters.'" Ale had been introduced as "orphan" in the past, a painful word to him. "So it was different hearing that," he said. "It changed my point of view...to start feeling like I belonged to a family."

While Ale and I were talking, two people crossed my peripheral vision and quietly sat in nearby chairs. It was Salvador, Ale's older brother, and Tia, Salvador's wife. They were newlyweds – married for five months. I invited them over to our table. Tia stayed for a minute and then went inside to visit with Gary and Sharon.

Ale was seven years old, and Salvador nine, when they moved into La Casa. I asked them about memories of being at Sonia's house.

"I remember that we shared beds, because there were not enough," Salvador said. "Half the roof was down. It was a pretty poor house. There were times that we lacked food. We went to a day care. We spent really good times there." He also remembered visits from the Powells, Larsons, and Napolis.

"It was awesome," Salvador said about living with so many other children. "It's a sense of community that you build. You get used to spending time with kids in the room. Play with them. I think it's something that I lack right now. Because I'm used to, all my life, living in a community." It was just him and Tia now.

"Sometimes I need noise, I need someone loud."

"I was always in trouble, so I cannot say the same thing," Ale chimed in and laughed.

"How have you experienced God's love through being at La Casa?" I asked.

"I think now we can see different ways that we can experience God, not only his love, but his provision, his protection," Ale said. "I remember this time the money was not coming through to La Casa. We only used to have beans and rice for meals. We were praying about getting money and food. And we went to school that day and when we came back, there was a family and their car was inside the garage. They started talking and when they opened the car, it was filled with cereal, powdered milk, rice, oil."

"The biggest experience about God while I was there...was when I met my dad again," Salvador said.

When he was young there was a team that visited La Casa, and on the last day of their visit they asked the kids if they had a prayer request.

"I didn't believe in God at that time. They were saying 'God is love' and in my head was this big struggle...I didn't want to hear them. Where is my mom? Why did she die so early? And all these crazy questions. I remember that I slept close to the window, I always like to see at night the stars. I was like, why am I here?"

A child beside him gave his own prayer request, which was to simply pray for his family. So, Salvador took his cue from him.

"And I say to this lady, 'Just pray for my dad.' I don't even remember what she said. They didn't translate for me. But I remember when she prayed and she hugged me and she said bye. And then we met our dad...again."

It had been years since the boys, who were then in their mid-teens, had seen their biological father. Out of the blue, their father had spoken with the courts in an attempt to find Ale and Salvador. The courts pointed him to La Casa.

Ale and Salvador were among the first La Casa kids to experience life in the transition home once they aged out of La Casa. It wasn't an easy change for them.

"To be independent...was something that we didn't know. That whole life living in a bubble, a good bubble, then going to the transition house. We didn't even know how to cook. Because they cooked it for us," Salvador said.

"The only thing we were doing was making our beds and cleaning the dining room," Ale said. "Dinner was the only time we were sweeping, mopping, washing dishes." They had full days that started with breakfast, going to school, coming home for lunch, resting, homework and then dinner. "You get used to having your houseparents."

"Houseparents" was a term often used when referring to the couples who lived in and managed the homes. But, even though their role in the children's lives was significant, the houseparents didn't replace the children's biological parents.

"It felt like living with houseparents when you go to college, I imagine," Salvador said. "You got a room in the university. They're there, but now you're making your own way."

Gerardo and Sandra would take the boys grocery shopping with them. Ale shared memories of shopping at PriceSmart, savoring sips of Coke and other food samples they gave to patrons. "At least we were prepared for how to do groceries," he said.

The young adults in the transition home were expected to either attend school or work. Ale studied culinary arts every day from 7 a.m. to 5 p.m. Salvador studied music for almost a year but decided to work instead. For his first job he simply showed up at the door of a local workshop that manufactured iron products like doors and windows. They hired him on the spot.

After Ale moved out of the transition house, he lived with his biological father for a few months. "It was really hard, because even though I knew that he was my dad, there was not a bond between us, dad to son," he said.

Ale began work as a Spanish–English translator and, eventually, both brothers ended up working together at an organization called YWAM (Youth with a Mission). YWAM mobilized local people to become missionaries in El Salvador as well as across the globe.

When I did my disciple training school in YWAM, we have a class that is called Father's Heart. In that moment, God speak to me and said, 'I heard that prayer that day.' Something that I didn't expect, I didn't even want it, because I was really hurt by him. But that was the biggest moment, because even when I thought that I didn't need it, to meet my dad, God knew that I needed to meet him again."

"Are there any challenges that we haven't talked about that you wish to share?" I asked.

"One of the biggest struggles, because I lived it, and probably whoever is living at La Casa, is your true identity," Ale said. "We grew up in a Christian orphanage, surrounded by Christian people, hearing God's Word, praying. But that doesn't make you a Christian. Until the moment you actually decide to make Jesus your Lord in your life, then you embrace your true identity. I was hiding my true feelings, until the moment I embraced that I had value, that I'm the son of God. I didn't grow up with my own parents, but God gave us a married couple who made that role all the time that we were there. I still call them mom and dad. God was taking care of me every single moment of my life when I was at La Casa."

"Mine was trusting people," Salvador said. A change in psychologists caused pain that ran deep for him. "Trying to let someone inside of me, and me be free to love them and say yeah, I trust you, I know you don't want anything bad for me. Then when you were reaching that point, pop, I'm leaving La Casa."

"When this new person came, I was like, I'm not going to talk to you like I was talking to her. That's not possible. But I wasn't even able to say, I'll give you a chance. Because for me it was hard. My parents abandoned me, and then them leaving or quitting. I don't want to feel this again. And I didn't understand that that's a season that is normal, some people come, some people leave. And finally I understand. In some ways I'm the person who comes to some place now that I'm doing missions, and then leaving. And I'm like, okay, I know, it's not their fault, it was my fault, at the time I was like that."

"You said you were tired of hearing about God and prayer. How did that change?" I asked Salvador.

"I think it changed when I was in the transition house," he said. "So many times I met with Gary, Gary's like, 'What are you doing? You're wasting your talent.' Because I was valedictorian in my class. I was working in the workshop, but at the end I was like, I'm lacking something."

Then Salvador met new houseparents who were working at La Casa. "When I met her, I don't know why, I feel that she's like my mom. I don't have any memory about my mom. And I called her mommy. And we got this relationship really close, with her husband as well. It was something beautiful."

"One day, I was like, I don't want to do anything anymore. They said, 'but you've got to keep working or they're going to kick you out of the transition house.' I was feeling alone. And I was walking through my bedroom and I was like, God, if you exist, will you give me something new. Something that will change my whole being. It was just a thought. It wasn't even a prayer. And I went to bed."

A few months later Salvador received the opportunity to work with YWAM. He objected at first, but eventually agreed to go and moved into the community there. At nineteen years old, he was the youngest in the disciple training school.

"I got there, and I remember when they started talking, I was like, I don't know if I want to believe what you're saying," Salvador said. "And my discipler said to me, 'I don't want to make you believe this. That's something *you* will do.' Even when it was six months [in] it was a challenge to believe. Knowing a God, knowing someone that will be mad if I do a mistake. And I started knowing a father suddenly. I was like wow, this cannot be God. This cannot be my Father. Because I always compared to my own father. I was like, I know you will abandon me. And even in my prayer time, He would give me Bible verses saying I will not leave you as an orphan.

"It was crazy seeing God's provision," Salvador said. "But it was something that started in La Casa. I used to cry at night a lot when I was there. Because I missed my family. And I remember waiting for everyone to fall asleep. Because I was one of the oldest. And then after I was sure they were sleeping, I would cry. God even said one time, 'I was there when you were crying.' And He didn't say it to me. Another person said it to me. I was like, what the heck is going on. In the middle of the prayer, I turned to him and was like, how do you know that? And he said, 'I don't know, God told me to tell you this, He was with you when you were crying.' Even in the moment, I was like, this is witchcraft. And he's like, 'No, it's God.' And he challenged me to take a moment, be quiet and listen to Him. And I started listening to these beautiful words like, 'You're my beloved son. And I'm really pleased with you. I'm proud of you. I know that it took you so long to come back to me, but finally you're here.' That changed my life. When I heard that, I was like, oh, you do talk. And I thought God was quiet my whole life. But actually He was always speaking, but I never listened."

To end our time together, I asked a final question. "Is there anything else that you want to share?"

"One of the best lessons that La Casa can give you is Jesus," Salvador said. "Even when we didn't want Him, He provided. And I am glad they never quit. Even when we were forced to go to youth group...they knew it would not be empty at the end. Something will grow. But even God in those memories, He's always like, 'Hey, don't forget that it wasn't them, it was me. It was always about me. Me and you together, we're more than only you apart.'"

Salvador and Ale had a falling-out at one point.

"La Casa believes in restoration of families," he said. "When [Ale] came back into my life, it was hard. Because we hurt each other. But now we're experiencing this restoration in our life and in our family. We spend afternoons just talking. We go on Sundays and play soccer together. Now we work together in the same organization. We're closer and closer and closer. I think that's something Gary believed first."

His words trailed off with a shift in thought.

"I don't know if Gary felt like he wanted to quit on us."

"He's probably had those moments," I said, and we all laughed.

"Because we weren't easy kids, either. But being with someone that always came and said, 'Hey, my son' and always talked the best about us, made me believe that I can be a better person."

"I said to my wife one day, 'Do you know what, my dream is coming true.' And she's like, 'What are you talking about?' We have a family now, I have a family, finally. I have my brother and my wife, working together. And that's something that God talked to me about a long time ago. And I was like, how will that be possible?"

Ale had a different perspective than Salvador, having lived at La Casa and also worked there as a tío. "I remember the first month [working there], it was horrible," Ale said. He struggled to work with some of his colleagues. But he learned valuable lessons at the same time.

The houseparents "taught me something that was real important...and that is we are pastors. What we preach and teach, that's what we have to live here at La Finca. Because you cannot talk with authority if you are not living it," he said.

"God gave me so many lessons through the kids when I was working then. Being at my age comparing to the kids' age, you can say, oh, I already went through that. It's kindergarten-level stuff. But when you realize that God has given you a new perspective, a new point of view, or that thing that you call simple or basic? You realize that your process is not done yet. Even though we are alumni from La Casa, we are still learning."

When Ale presented his resignation letter to La Casa, he met with Ceferino first, the house dad for the boys' home, and then with Gary.

"Gary was just listening to me the whole time. I was like, I just want to leave this place. And I remember...the first thing he said was, 'You know I can talk to you like a boss to his employee. But I'm not going to talk to you like that. I'm going to talk to you like a father to his son.' I think part of the men we have become until now is through those people God put in the right place in the right moment in our life.

"Something I always say is, never say to a kid who lives in an orphanage, 'I understand you,' if your whole life you have been living with your parents. Why? Because it's a huge difference – living with people that you don't know, that you're not attached to. But...I believe now that God put them in our lives for so many reasons. Back [then] I didn't see it, but now I can see it."

Chapter 16

Sacred Trust

IN 2002, Aubrey Knight was the program director for a medical residency in Roanoke, Virginia. For six years prior he led medical mission teams to Bolivia, that included other doctors and residents from the program. His wife, Esther, and their teenage daughter and son often accompanied him.

In May of that year their trip to Bolivia, scheduled for August, was thrown a curve ball. The airline tripled the price of tickets from what was originally agreed upon, making the trip cost prohibitive for the team. Aubrey scrambled to find an alternate solution.

He and Gary Powell were friends and had been in recent contact. Aubrey's daughter was headed into her sophomore year of college and making plans to assist with earthquake relief in El Salvador the following spring. Neither Aubrey nor his family had been to El Salvador before. So, Aubrey called him.

It was Friday night on May 17, just hours before the kids living in the abandoned warehouse would be moved into their new home and La Casa de mi Padre would officially open its doors.

"Gary, I've got a medical team, we're kind of at a loss. We don't have anywhere to go. Would there be something for us to do if we came down to El Salvador in two months?" Aubrey asked.

Gary had often encouraged Aubrey to visit El Salvador. So, he invited the medical team to see the La Casa children. He also suggested it might bless the people living in the community they'd been working with, helping to rebuild houses demolished by the earthquake.

The medical trip to El Salvador was set in motion.

"In my mind...this was a one-year thing," Aubrey said, regarding that first visit. "We were going to go back to Bolivia the next year."

I listened on the phone, now back home in the United States, as Aubrey shared his story.

"So we get there and the place, the people, the kids, everything about the work that was going on...all of it was so compelling and we were so drawn to what God seemed to be doing both around us but to us in that trip, that Esther and I said this isn't a one-year thing. We're going to go back."

They didn't intend to go to El Salvador with their daughter while she served there the next spring, but they couldn't stay away.

"We go back in March and it's remarkable that in six to seven short months, how much better the kids were, how much healthier...how much God had blessed this ministry that was started on a shoestring. Clearly a major step of faith for all the folks that were involved in this, without any sense as to how it was going to be maintained. It was just so evident – God's provision, God's protection. His presence in that place was so palpable, so clear. And so real. It was just like this magnet. We couldn't not continue to be involved in that."

Sixteen years had passed since that first trip, and the Knights hadn't returned to Bolivia yet. Instead, they took every opportunity to visit La Casa. They traveled back at least once a year, sometimes more.

I asked Aubrey to recall some of his findings when he first examined the children. He told the story of a six-month-old boy.

"He had no muscle tone whatsoever. He couldn't sit up without someone sitting him up. He couldn't hold his head up. I said to myself, *This kid will never walk*." Aubrey had predicted severe delays in his physical development and the need for multiple wheelchairs as the boy grew.

"When we came back in March, he was walking at thirteen months old. There are some extremely healthy, even precocious, children who don't walk at thirteen months. But he was walking. I think that was God telling me, *He's my child who, yes, has gotten off to a rough start, but I love him and am able to do things that according to your finite clinical mind, can't be done*." Aubrey paused. "Don't get me wrong. I teach medical knowledge, and I teach evidence-based medicine. But I also am someone who does recognize that there are things that we can't explain."

As I write this, that boy is now a teenager and physically strong. Aubrey still keeps a picture of him from that six-month visit. "It's not like it's framed and something I look at every day, but I know where to find it if I need it. Because I need it to remind myself that we serve an amazingly powerful God that does inexplicable things on occasion. And [that boy] is inexplicable."

That first medical team to visit La Casa was small – around fifteen people including four doctors, Aubrey's immediate family, and a Spanish teacher, among others. They arrived during the middle of the week, so their plan was to see the children on Thursday and Friday, and then see patients in the community of Santo Tomás on Monday and Tuesday.

At La Casa, they secured the boys' bedroom as the area for doctors to see patients. Someone recorded vital signs and then the doctors would see the children individually. There was ample time to spend with each one. Medical records were created that could be handed to local physicians – the US doctors were not intended to be the children's main doctors. Their only goal was to perform initial assessments to help the La Casa staff understand how to meet physical needs.

The doctors were able to see all the children that Thursday, which left Friday open. So, the team decided to visit Santo Tomás ahead of schedule. But Aubrey wasn't expecting what happened when they opened their temporary medical clinic.

"The most important thing that you can know about a mission trip is flexibility," Aubrey said. He was a self-professed over-planner who created spreadsheets to limit surprises as much as possible. In spite of that, he emphasized "being sensitive to God's leading and when you feel like you're supposed to change the plan."

Then he added, "One of the first people to show up was a woman who had a blanket in her arms, and clearly something wrapped up in the blanket. And she opened up the blanket and there was a week-old infant that was barely alive. The baby was born in the hospital, and when they left, they gave her this bottle of infant vitamins. It's a dropper bottle, and they told her, 'Give this child one drop per day.' And that's all she was giving the child. He was getting no nutrition whatsoever because she misunderstood that he also needs to be eating. This is not his food."

The boy was transferred to a local Christian ministry for malnourished children. There he was dropper-fed because he didn't have the strength or ability to swallow. After a period of critical care, he survived.

"He would not have been alive on Monday. There's no doubt in my mind. I'm not sure he would've been alive if he had come after lunch instead of getting there before lunch," Aubrey said.

Seeing patients out in the community was different from seeing the kids at La Casa. Crowd control and triage were necessary due to the large volume of people that would arrive. The doctors had to work quickly to ensure everyone had the opportunity to be seen. And just as with the La Casa kids, they were not the main doctors for the community. They acted as an urgent care center for that moment in time only.

The teams always visited communities recommended by La Casa, with the team's safety and security in mind. While La Casa often emphasized that teams were not the target of gang-related activity, it was wise to steer clear of unfamiliar territory. In recent years, the medical teams have exclusively met with the community immediately surrounding La Casa's property – to bless La Casa's neighbors and build relationships with them.

"It's the same people, so we've got to know them pretty well," Aubrey said. "I recognize the folks as they come in. And you see kids grow up, grow older. And you see older women become widows. It's been fulfilling and also enlightening to watch that process."

Aubrey's time in El Salvador now flowed into his everyday practice.

"I'm not sure I used to talk about medicine being a calling...to serve those who come to us. Just as the children arrive at La Casa broken and vulnerable and hurting, every person who walks through the front door of my office, in one way or another, is broken and vulnerable," he said. "I've heard things from people that I'm pretty sure I'm the only person who knows that. That is a sacred trust that we have. They are trusting us to provide some relief from the suffering that they're faced with."

Chapter 17

Better Together

IN 1977, Gary Niebur's mother passed away one week after his sixteenth birthday. Her loss caused him to ask soul-searching questions like, *Is there a God?* and, *Where did she go?* Through a youth group he attended, he found answers to his questions by placing his faith in Christ.

Each morning, he woke up at 4:00 a.m. to deliver newspapers on his daily route. While he tossed papers onto driveways, he listened to the radio. One morning, a commercial about sponsoring a child in another country caught his attention. So, he sponsored a child in India.

Niebur was on his high school speech and debate team. For a persuasive-speaking competition, he wrote a speech on why and how to sponsor a child in a developing country. Through his research and writing, his dream to do something more, began.

At age seventeen, he read the autobiography of George Müller. He was so inspired by what he read, that he started saving money toward the dream of building an orphanage, as Müller did. He began small – he rolled coins and set them aside. Then, he continued saving money through his teen years and into adulthood, through major life changes like starting a family and working professionally.

He married Teresa and they had three daughters – Sarah Gail, Lily, and Sophia. Niebur became a world-ranked tennis professional, competing in Wimbledon, and eventually co-founded Stan Smith Events. As the success of Stan Smith Events grew, he established a charitable trust account, as his family was able to save larger amounts toward his dream.

He began thinking about specific places where an orphanage might be built – somewhere that was a nonstop flight from Atlanta. Perhaps Central America – he had studied Spanish and played tennis in Mexico while he was in college. He envisioned a place where people could travel outside the United States, connect with the children, serve, and have fun together.

One day, more than twenty years after he first started saving, Teresa made a bold statement to her husband.

"I think we've saved enough," she said.

He hesitated. "We haven't found the right place."

That would soon change.

His father had passed away in the early 2000s and, with money separate from the trust account, he wanted to do something to honor him. He considered building a playground or small pool for children. He started working with an organization in El Salvador, but his plans to build there never solidified.

Then, he received a phone call from his long-time friend Eddie Staub – the founder of the children's home that was mentoring La Casa de mi Padre. At that point, Eagle Ranch and La Casa had been working together for eight years. And, La Casa was at a critical stage in its development. They needed more funding to continue growing.

"You need to meet Gary and Sharon and La Casa de mi Padre," Eddie said, "they have this land."

Eddie connected Niebur with the Powells, which quickly led to a meaningful relationship. Niebur and his business partner, Stan Smith, knowing how important soccer is in Latin American culture, decided to donate funds for La Casa to build a soccer field at the farm. When the field was complete, it was close to Niebur's youngest daughter Sophia's tenth birthday. She was given the opportunity to go anywhere in the world, a tenth birthday tradition in their family.

"Dad, I know your dream has been to do this," Sophia said, as she chose El Salvador as the place to celebrate her birthday.

They went down to dedicate the soccer field on their first visit to La Casa. Sophia's friend, Bailey, and her father, Bill Willits, traveled with them. Bill was Niebur's friend and one of the founding members of North Point Ministries. Bill would be a sounding board for Niebur, as he processed whether La Casa would be the place to give the money he'd been saving for more than half his life.

"It was amazing," Niebur said and grinned, his blue eyes turned to the side as he remembered the dedication ceremony. "Seeing the kids' faces. They had no idea they were getting a soccer field. No one had told them."

Niebur and I were on a video call, it was February 2021, and he became more animated as he described that day in December 2009. He had a big bright smile.

"Adidas donated shorts, shirts, shoes, soccer balls. And we dressed the kids in all the uniforms," he said as he grinned again.

Stan Smith has strong ties to the sports brand, Adidas. Stan is a former World No. 1, US Open and Wimbledon Champion, with the iconic Adidas shoe named after him. It's through their close relationship that Adidas participated in La Casa's vision, too.

The soccer field is accessible just off the main road through the farm. But, it isn't immediately visible. It sits down off the side of a cliff, with a long series of steps traversing the hillside.

"They cut the ribbon, and the kids all ran to the edge and looked over and just couldn't believe it."

He shifted thoughts quickly.

"The biggest aha moment for me was...Gary [Powell] had us over and invited five of the kids. It was three family members and two family members. They were the older kids," he said, holding up three fingers on one hand and two on the other.

"So we sat together. And they shared their story of how" – his throat grew tight, his voice quieted –"how God had forgiven them, so they decided to forgive their parents for the abuse that they had gone through. That as a result of La Casa, they were able to do that."

Niebur then sought counsel on the decision that brought him to El Salvador.

"I talked to Bill and said, 'What do you think?' And he confirmed, this is good. This is probably the right thing."

When they returned to the States, the Niebur family donated their savings to La Casa de mi Padre. Along with other funds raised by generous donors, it would eventually help La Casa build one of their first homes on the farm, the "Hope" home. Bill's experience there also led to North Point Ministries becoming a partner of La Casa through their global(x)[17] program.

Those relationships would have a significant impact on the future of La Casa and their ability to help at-risk children in El Salvador. But Niebur emphasized more than once that the success of La Casa wasn't determined by a single person or partnership.

"This is my life...the fulfillment of a vision and dream. But, it's really how everybody has come alongside the mission and done so much."

By 2021, La Casa's supporters were located far and wide, from the staff who worked there each day, the organization's board, strategic mentors, donors within Latin America and across the United States, to teams who visited and served at La Casa.

For the first time, La Casa had an emergency fund to leverage during seasons when giving was down. Niebur credited Eddie's wise counsel for that.

"You *need* this emergency fund," he remembered him saying.

La Casa was also experiencing unprecedented growth in several areas.

"La Casa is better than it's ever been, *by far*," he said, now as a serving member of the board.

This he credited, in part, to Aubrey Knight, who was now the Board Chair. Aubrey led the way in uniting two separate boards that previously oversaw La Casa.

"As a result of that, giving is up. Confidence is up. Trust is up," Niebur said.

"One of my key strengths is to connect people into relationships - with one another and to God. Then, they build trust within those relationships and it transforms their lives. La Casa's been a part of it."

One week later in March 2021, I logged back into Zoom to speak with Jeff Foote, vice chair of La Casa de mi Padre's board. Jeff had been married to Jackie for over thirty-one years, and they had two grown sons, Jake and Luke.

Jeff was casually dressed, wearing a TCU hat and George

Mason University jacket. He wore eyeglasses with thin, metal frames. When he spoke his voice was smooth, like a well-played instrument.

Throughout his professional career, Jeff had the opportunity to travel the world. So, in 2011, when his sons were fifteen and twelve years old, he wanted them to experience life outside of Atlanta, Georgia, where they lived. Both boys had studied Spanish in school, so Central America was a natural choice. That summer, they were accepted on a family trip to serve with La Casa de mi Padre through global(x).

Jeff reflected on his love for soccer – he played the sport for twenty-five years. In high school he had the opportunity to play in Mexico for two weeks with his soccer team. He considered himself a "decent" player, but was in awe of what he witnessed at La Casa.

"I was amazed to see these youngsters in El Salvador that were incredibly skilled. One was Jansen Gomez. I think he was fourteen years old. All I could think was...the ball is a magnet on this kid," he said.

Jeff's son, Jake, was just a year older than Jansen. Jake was also a big-time soccer fan and he and Jansen became fast friends, bonding over their shared interest. When their time in El Salvador was finished, Jake asked his parents a poignant question.

"We were sitting on the plane to go home after being there for a week, and Jake said, 'Can we come back next year?' Jackie and I kind of looked at each other. And Jake said, 'Well, Jansen said, "I'll see you next year."' And, of course, Jackie and I are both gobsmacked and said, 'Well, *yeah*, I guess we *have* to.'" He laughed.

After that trip, the Foote family made a commitment to stay involved with La Casa – to pray for the staff and children, to support them financially, and to serve. The next year they went back on another global(x) trip, this time as leaders.

"So we got to see Jansen again, and play fútbol again, and build more of a relationship with the kids. And I think that's part of the heart and beauty of La Casa is that, Gary and Sharon really hope that you're going to create a relationship with the kids. And with the organization as well. I think they do a really good job of leading people to that," he said.

In late 2013, Jeff joined La Casa's board.

"An important thing I want to convey is in El Salvador, when a kid turns eighteen, if they're in some sort of foster home or orphanage, they can no longer be in that setting. They have to go out on their own. A marvelous thing of La Casa is that they have this program that's called the Bridge. As long as you're working hard, your grades are good...you can continue on there. So, as Jansen was turning eighteen, he felt that he wanted to go into that program."

Soon after Jansen moved into the transition home, as he waited in a park area to catch a bus, gang members threatened him and shoved him around. The attack sparked a strong emotional response.

"I think [Jansen] was under a lot of peer pressure about what to do. Does he drop out of school. He didn't like school. Wants to be a professional fútbol player, but how do you do that. So, I think he was being recruited to join the gang. And Gary Powell called me and told me that he was very concerned about that. And, by that time, we had developed more of a relationship, Jansen and I. So, Jake and I decided, let's go down in June of 2014, and let's spend a bunch of time with Jansen, just the two of us. You guys are the same age."

Jeff joked that he was the first board member to personally rent a car in San Salvador and drive around. Remembering my own experiences as a passenger in San Salvador traffic, I thought he was brave.

"We definitely got lost right off the bat, but we made it." Jeff grinned.

"So, we spent a whole bunch of time with Jansen. We visited his school. It was right in the middle of the World Cup 2014 in Brazil, perfect for the three of us to watch games on TV. We went to some restaurants and watched some games, we watched some games at La Casa. It was a really great bonding time. Our goal was to deepen our relationship with him, and our goal was to say" – Jeff's voice softened as he leaned forward – "'We care about you. People love you. And listen...'" – his voice softened even more as he smiled – "'you *can't* join a gang. You've got to finish school. We're supportive of you.' His eyes turned red. "And it struck me, that, this is my *son*. This is my son from El Salvador. It's my responsibility to give him some coaching, some mentoring, some guidance. And, I believe in him."

Jeff's love for Jansen was palpable.

"So, yeah, the kid graduated, I think in 2015. He graduated from high school. He's a leader at the Bridge. He does things, still, at La Casa on the farm. I'm immensely proud of him."

Jeff also shared about Jonathan, Jansen's younger brother. Through La Casa, Jonathan was given the opportunity to attend a soccer camp in Buenos Aires, Argentina. Though Jeff's relationship with Jonathan was not as close, his support of both brothers was clear.

"I wish I knew Jonathan better."

Then, he gave another glimpse into his relationship with Jansen.

"I get texts from Jansen, where he'll send me a note and say, 'Hey dad, I love you.' or 'I love you so much. How are you?' type of thing. I sent him a couple notes this morning, just to see, How are you? How's work? Did you vote?"

We laughed. Then he echoed the excellence he had witnessed in La Casa during his ten years of involvement.

"There are constantly new difficulties thrown at them. Whether it's weather-related, government-related, gang-related, COVID-related...they tackle them with grace. They grow from it and get better."

Chapter 18

Joy

"GOOOD MOOOORNING," Sharon said in a melodic voice. "How are you?"

It was August 18, 2021, more than three years since I first interviewed Sharon for the book. I was sitting inside my home office, connected with Sharon via Zoom. Her camera was turned off, so I assumed she didn't want to be seen on camera that day. I totally got it.

I answered her question tentatively. Chad and I had just found out that we had possible exposure to COVID-19, so that was consuming my thoughts that morning. La Casa had been hard-hit by the virus – Sharon explained some of the challenges they were facing.

While she was talking, she paused mid-sentence. Suddenly, her camera came alive.

"Oh, I didn't have my video on," Sharon said.

Gary was standing beside her, his hand pulling away from

the computer screen. He made a funny face at the camera and wrapped his arm around her as we laughed. It made me happy to see them in front of me.

She wore a pretty black sleeveless top with gathers on the front and small ruffles around the edges. Her eyeglasses had dark framing around the tops of the lenses. He was wearing a blue and white checkered shirt.

"Hi, Christina, how are you?" Gary asked.

He joined the conversation for a brief moment before bowing out. Sharon and I finished talking about COVID and then moved on to our reason for meeting: to talk more about La Casa for the writing of this book.

A third home now existed on the farm. Like the other two homes, it had its own unique story for how it came to be, one that included a famous singer/songwriter.

"We got this Facebook message, I believe is what it was originally, saying, 'We're an organization, we're looking for projects in El Salvador, can we contact you?' And then we got an email, and I ignored them all. I was like, *nobody* comes to you and says I want to do something." Sharon's face had a look of disbelief as she laughed and continued the story.

"I was like, this is weird. This is a scam. *I'm* not going to get La Casa involved in this scam." She gestured her hands to mimic a wall as she said her next words in staccato, like a judge delivering the final say in a court ruling. "I'm. Protecting. Its. Name." Her contagious laugh grew even bigger.

"Then they called on the phone and talked to Catherina. And Catherina said" – her voice became soft and humble – "'Sharon, I think this...is legit. They've given me their website.'"

The organization that contacted them was the Maestro Cares Foundation (MCF), co-founded by Marc Anthony. Their mission is to build homes and schools for disadvantaged children in Latin America and the United States.[18]

"So we met with them," Sharon continued, "I think it was a Sunday afternoon, Gary and I at Shaw's[19], there on the balcony, had some gelato together. And what was supposed to be a less-than-an-hour meeting, three hours later we were in the car and taking them to see the property. We just clicked. We just knew in our hearts that something was stirring. I think God was confirming it."

After the meeting, several weeks passed before they heard back from MCF. When they did, MCF extended an offer to help build the third home, with additional funds provided by a local partner.

"How they [MCF] work is they look for an in-country sponsor or business or foundation, something to come along and put the other half in," Sharon said. "What they're trying to do is increase local awareness of the programs that are running within the country," she said, which helps encourage social responsibility at that level.

For this project MCF chose to partner with SISTEMA FEDE-CRÉDITO (SF), an organization similar to a credit union in the States. Before La Casa's board agreed to start building, however, they had one major concern.

Sharon made the sound of squealing brakes as she leaned back in her chair. "We just opened two homes and...we don't feel like we're financially sound there to add something else on. Like, what if we lost it all because we were too anxious and jumped ahead," Sharon said.

"So our board said, we need to raise the money for one year's operating costs before we even begin." She paused slightly. "And I think our hearts sunk a little bit, like, God's *working*, He's provided this that we didn't even know about. I think for us it was more of, a bit of faith or trust, but they also were being wise, very wise," she said and smiled.

"So that took almost a year but God *provided*. Operating costs for a whole year. Maestro Cares put up, I think almost a quarter of it, FEDECRÉDITO said they would put up part of it, and then other donors chipped in. So, we pulled together and had the money to know that when the home was completed, we'd have one year's operating costs to hopefully let La Casa catch up in fundraising and to be able to sustain the home long-term."

It was 2019 when they built the third home – the "Joy" home – and La Casa held a special dedication ceremony. Marc Anthony sent a video of himself, sharing his well-wishes for the children. The home was ready to embrace eight more girls who needed love and care.

The year 2020 was unlike any La Casa had seen before. Thanks to COVID-19, schools were closed and La Casa was forced to pivot to online education for the children. That revealed more challenges like not having a steady internet connection at the farm. They tried to use cellular hot spots and even climbed trees in an effort to get a better signal.

There weren't enough computers for the children. Sometimes, teachers would unexpectedly announce a Zoom class was starting in fifteen minutes, giving La Casa little time to print out the necessary paperwork for everyone who needed it. On top of that, La Casa's education coordinator lived in a community whose bus service had been shut down, so she wasn't able to get to the farm.

The virus spread through La Casa, severely impacting both the children and staff alike. La Casa had to get creative on how to continue operating among widespread illnesses, quarantines, and staff shortages. Every person on staff who was available and able-bodied, regardless of their position, had to jump in and help the children with their day-to-day activities and schoolwork. That meant removing the focus from other key areas in the organization.

"It was a really hard year," Sharon said.

When 2021 arrived, schools were still online and La Casa couldn't sustain that model. So, they prayed about what to do. And as with each time they'd faced adversity in the past, something beautiful was waiting for them on the horizon.

La Casa had a fill-in tía in one of the homes who mentioned that she knew of a few places that managed homeschools locally. This surprised La Casa, as they previously believed that was illegal in El Salvador. However, through research, they discovered a small local homeschool that was recognized by the government. Gang activity in that area made homeschooling the only viable option.

After speaking with the homeschool, La Casa joined their program and hired five teachers for what they call "on-site schooling." The teachers travel to the farm to teach classes, using curriculum based on that of the accredited homeschool. The children complete lessons and their work gets evaluated. During each grading period, La Casa's education coordinator submits all of the documentation and grades – proof that the children did the work – which ultimately gets reported to the government and the children receive credit.

The new system means the children can learn to think more critically and receive hands-on education. Now when they study plants, they explore plants growing on the farm and slice them open for a closer look.

In the afternoons, the houseparents teach electives. The children learn about physical education, drama, music, art, and even cooking. An extra benefit is that the children get to see the houseparents in a more fun setting vs. solely as the ones who manage the home.

The schedules for the houseparents and the children are much more relaxed, too. Now that the various trips to outside schools have been eliminated, the children can start their mornings a little later and still have enough time to get ready for class. Then at lunchtime, the kids can simply walk back home where they eat together as a family and debrief, before going to class again in the afternoon. It's also allowed for less homework, which means there aren't as many late nights as there were before.

"It's been beautiful to see the confidence that's come about, the enthusiasm," Sharon said. "Not that you don't have hurdles, and you still don't have kids struggling, you're always going to have that. But overall, they have a different perception of what school is, what education is, what learning can *be*."

There was passion in her voice as she described the rote learning the children were exposed to in their previous schools vs. how they now received education in the on-site school.

"It's been the best thing we've ever done," Sharon said. "Our kids are flourishing. They get up in the morning *excited* to go to school."

Chapter 19

Break the Chain

WHEN FRANCISO "FRANK" MAGAÑA APPEARED on my computer screen, I asked him how he was doing, and he swung his device around to give me a panoramic view of the others in the room. Daniela, Luis, and Elba were there inside the transition home, working on a puzzle at the table. They smiled and waved and I loved catching the surprise glimpse of them. It was mid-January 2022, when La Casa was approaching their twentieth anniversary.

Frank left the table, his screen bobbing up and down as he walked.

"Sorry," he said with a boyish laugh. I squinted my eyes so I wouldn't get motion sick.

He soon sat back in a comfortable chair. He was wearing a short-sleeved shirt with dark gray, red, and white stripes, his black hair shorter on the sides than it was on top. Frank is Whitney's husband and, like her, works with La Casa.

At the start of our talk, he shared experiences that foreshadowed his work with the ministry. He was born in El Salvador to a Christian family and, in his teens, served as an English–Spanish translator within his church, for teams that would visit from Missouri.

When he was trying to decide what to study in college, though, assessment tests gave inconclusive results three different times. Overall, they pointed to art, music, and theater as subjects to lean toward, and analysis and math as ones to avoid. He wondered if God had a different idea, though.

"I was sitting down at the admissions office and I prayed. I said, 'Jesus, guide me to that degree that I'm going to *suck* at.'" He paused for a few seconds as he held my gaze.

I smiled because I was accustomed to his quirky humor, but sensed he was going somewhere important with that statement. That, and he assured me he wasn't lying.

"Because if I succeed," he continued, "then I will be able to say it was because of *your* grace and not my own."

So, at age seventeen, as he eyed a list of potential degrees in front of him, he chose the one that combined everything he shouldn't pursue: economics.

That decision led to a challenging first year of college with "a lot of faith, a lot of prayer, and hours and hours at the library... trying to learn," he said. And learn, he did.

He became so successful in his studies that he was accepted into a different school in Chile which, according to Frank, has the best economic faculty in Latin America, and where only the top 3 percent of high school graduates are accepted. He spent three years there.

"But that was the most humbling experience because I was so full of pride," he said with a serious tone in his voice. He chose to be far away from his family, something that wasn't common in El Salvador, and was lonely.

After graduation, he was hired as a university research coordinator, for a program that served outstanding students from public schools.

It was a "wonderful experience working with their parents, and seeing kids ride buses for four hours, getting up at 3 a.m. every weekend for six years, to get a scholarship for university. I was witnessing these things. I was learning about them. It was a beautiful thing."

After a while, Frank left the university to work in investment banking, where he applied his economics degree doing market analysis and fund management. He found success there, too, in his five years in the industry.

"But I didn't feel fulfilled. I felt...empty," he said.

During that time, he started serving on the worship team at Union Church, and began dating Whitney. He also became involved with La Casa from a volunteer standpoint. He held Bible studies on Sundays with those in the transition home, and helped them clean the house.

"I spent a couple of years praying to God for the opportunity to just go back to my younger days, like when I was a translator for missionaries...and use my energy to serve Him."

His prayers were answered in 2016–2017, when Gary and Sharon entrusted Whitney and Frank with La Casa's finances while they were away on sabbatical, and offered him a formal position to oversee the transition home.

I asked if there was a specific story he wanted to share about his experiences with La Casa. He tilted his back for several seconds before answering.

"I would look at the transition home and all the young adults that pass through. To see those few, that, with hard work, faith, struggles, they finish their vocation, their degrees, or high school, or a small course. When they achieve these...milestones...to sit down with them and say, '*This* is how you break the chain. Because you're not repeating the story of your family.'"

The three young people, piecing the puzzle together in the other room, were living examples of that.

"Tell me about a time you've seen God's presence at La Casa," I said.

"That day that Jason found all these...maggots all over the house..."

My stomach turned as we laughed.

"One morning he sent me these pictures of all these fly maggots, crawling" – he grimaced and his voice fell to a whisper – "all over the floor."

"In the kitchen?"

"The kitchen, the living room, the study area. I'm talking about a very...bad situation. And we were able to clean that up and I would say, that's God's grace. Because they were even behind the walls." He laughed again.

Frank commented how he enjoys not having to sit behind a desk for work. He typically spends half his time at the farm and the other half at the transition home.

"But the truth is, this is nonstop. There's no actual schedule. I just see it as life, not as work."

I asked if Gary and Sharon, when they were ready to retire, were going to transition La Casa over to him and Whitney.

"Well, as an economist, I tend to think in terms of assumptions," Frank said. "I hate to assume in this specific aspect. Because in God's kingdom, you just can't walk life expecting that this outcome" – he gestured with his hands – "is just going to happen. I don't know. And that way of approaching my day-to-day life gives me a lot of peace. My only prayer is if...he feels that we are the right couple, then amen. We're going to take the role for as long as he finds us fit. If he feels there is a different couple or...person who has the right heart...to take up this role, then we are going to be here to serve [them]."

I asked Frank for final thoughts.

"I pray that my children are involved as much as they can [be] with La Casa." Frank and Whitney now have a young son. "Because if we really believe in this model, if we are really convinced that this can help somebody...I want them in."

Epilogue

AS WITH EVERY ministry and organization, the loving people involved ebb and flow.

Ceferino and Rosa Elena, and Juan Carlos and Milagro, are no longer serving as houseparents with La Casa; others have stepped in to fill their shoes. At the time of this writing, Henry and Astrid oversee the Grace home, and Brandon and Sara, the Hope home. But I was lucky enough to catch Rosa Elena on a trip to La Casa in December 2021, where she was helping with the annual Christmas party for La Casa's neighbors.

The girls in the newest home, the Joy home, receive love, time, and attention from their houseparents, Guillermo and Karol. Sarai is no longer on staff with La Casa but is enjoying life with her new husband. In early 2022, Serenity Therapeutic Riding Center broke ground for a new stable – the first complete structure in its history – built from brick and made to last.

Daniela finished her degree in psychology in 2021 and is pouring back into La Casa by working as a residential assistant in the transition home. Salvador moved to Canada with his wife, Tia. They have a young son, and Salvador went back to school. Likewise, Alejandro has since married. And Silvia, who was the girl that surprised everyone by stepping up to the microphone when they purchased the farm, is now the kindergarten teacher for La Casa.

On several occasions I've heard Gary and Sharon talk about

the "tapestry" that God has created, of his weaving people into their lives – people that come and go and help paint this big beautiful picture that no one can possibly imagine until they see it come to life. As I reflect on the stories told here, I can't help but get caught up in that imagery myself.

This book contains a snapshot in time. In reality, the story of La Casa de mi Padre continues today.

"God's placed a lot of people in our lives at just the opportune times. Maybe we were praying about them, and maybe even people we would have expected to jump in," Sharon told me, laughing briefly, "and answer whatever prayer, wasn't the way that God chose...I think to continuously remind us that *He's* the one writing this story."

Acknowledgments

WHEN I FIRST STARTED WRITING THIS BOOK, I was overwhelmed. I wouldn't have called myself a writer – period – and had never written a book. But now that it's done, I can say finishing this book is one of the most challenging and rewarding things I've ever done. Somewhere along the way my writing muscles grew stronger, to where I consider myself a serious writer today. It's as if God knew what He was doing when He planted the seed, before I thought I was ready.

Day by day, word by word, I've sensed His guidance and assurance that the book would be ready right on time, with His stories filling the pages. I'm thankful for His love that never fails.

Even though I've written the words in this book, the stories began long before I became involved with La Casa de mi Padre. I'm just grateful that, in a small way, my life has intersected with theirs. I'm also convinced I have the best people in my life who helped make this book a reality.

To Chad – I'm beyond thankful for our life together. I admire the way you lead and teach others, and I never stop learning from you. Thank you for loving me, for better and for worse, and always making space for creativity to bloom.

To Mom and Dad – thanks for giving me life...and your unconditional love ever since.

To Nasario, Scottie, Hannah, Grandma, Rachel, Jim, Cindy, Matt, Sara, and the rest of my family - it's finished! Thank you for your love and encouragement, even if it was just to say, "I can't wait to read it." It kept me going.

Extra thanks to Hannah for proofreading the layout, too.

To the children of La Casa de mi Padre, past and present – you bless everyone who knows you. That became even more apparent as I listened to stories for this book. You are a light, making a way for today and for future generations.

To the staff and regular volunteers of La Casa de mi Padre – the role you play in the children's lives is significant. Loving others is your specialty. I'm honored to witness it.

To Wendy Aguirre, Hilda Alvarado, Scott Anderson and Dawn Forbes, Alejandro Barahona, Salvador Barahona, Carmen de Jesús Rivera de Cruz, Sarai Cotto de Díaz, Jeff Foote, Ceferino and Rosa Elena González, Aubrey Knight, Dale and Christy Larson, Francisco and Whitney Magaña, Catherina Forero Mejia, Joseph and Jan Napoli, Gary Niebur, Loli Perez, Gary and Sharon Powell, Daniela Romero, Juan Carlos and Milagro Soto, Eddie Staub, David Torres – who shared their time, hearts, and stories with me (and meals, too) – thank you for trusting me. It was an honor to hear about what God has done in your life. An author learns more than what gets included in the final manuscript, so I hope I've handled your stories well. Thank you, again, from the bottom of my heart.

Extra thanks to Gary and Sharon, who were gracious hosts while I gathered stories in El Salvador. They invited me into their home, fed me food that went straight to my soul, drove me around town, and translated for others. They've answered many questions along the way. Also, thanks for proofreading the manuscript and giving valuable feedback.

And extra thanks to Jeff, who, when I told him I hadn't landed on the title for the book yet, said, "I think you have it – The Miracle Farm." It clicked. Sometimes the obvious isn't so obvious.

To Francisco and Patricia Magaña – thank you for carefully

translating this book into Spanish. I'll be forever grateful for you.

To Claudia Meyer – for your gifts of proofing the Spanish edition of this book and your industry expertise, thank you.

To Susan Burtch and Bev Anglin – who encouraged me to go and serve with La Casa de mi Padre the first time. I never imagined how much my heart and life would change because you cared enough to nudge me out of my comfort zone. Thank you for being living examples of what it means to trust God and love others well.

To Andy Stanley, global(x), North Point Community Church, and Browns Bridge Church – for 22 years you've inspired me and Chad to follow Jesus, and our lives are better for it. Thank you for your partnership with La Casa de mi Padre and for making it easy for others to be part of what God's doing there.

To Kristina Lappin – thank you for your heart, time, and encouragement you've given throughout this writing process, and the many meals we've shared together. I felt confident placing the early (and late!) manuscript in your hands – your thoughtful feedback made this book better. I'm grateful you were my teammate on that first trip to El Salvador.

To Moon DeSetto, Patrice Larson, and Mona Robertson – I've lost count of how many times you've asked how the book is going. Thank you for your love and affirmation. I'll treasure your friendship for a lifetime.

Extra thanks to Moon for the beautiful author photo, too.

To Chuck Blevins, Colleen Jones, Tracy Ann Nash, Christel Shuler, and Sara Steward – thanks for jumping in quickly and giving thoughtful feedback when I needed it. And, thanks for your encouragement (always).

To Liz Jones – who knew serving in El Salvador together would lead to four years of InsideOut? You've been my sounding board for many things, and I'll never be able to thank you enough for your friendship, care, and good advice from Day 1 of this writing project (and then some).

To my InsideOut students at Browns Bridge Church – I've been working on this book almost as long as we've known each other. To publish it the year you graduate feels serendipitous. It's been an honor watching you mature into bright, caring young ladies. It's given me fuel to keep writing, knowing that God is for you just as much as He is for the children of La Casa.

To all my global(x)/InsideOut teammates – it's been an honor to serve with you in El Salvador and gain a new perspective of the love of God, together.

To those who have supported me on a trip to El Salvador, in one way or another – thank you.

To Julane Fisher – a local author who met with me inside a Starbucks café at the very start of this project, sharing her expertise on the writing world. I didn't have a clue what I was doing, so thank you for showing me what was possible and for pointing me in the right direction. Thanks to Karen Pugh for the introduction, too.

To Joe and Ashley Shugart – thank you for the gift of a gorgeous book cover and layout. What a loving way to use your talents to honor God...and Steve. He'd be so pleased. And extra thanks for referring me to Elizabeth Hildreth, who helped with the layout of the Spanish edition.

To Christy Callahan – good books can't exist without good editors. Thank you for combing through each word and giving expert suggestions. Thank you for coaching me through the publishing process, too!

To Julie Hebert, Leah Judway, Jannell Palms, and Christel Shuler (again) – because friends like you have left lasting impressions on me, by your love for others and your creativity. I've carried you into the writing of this book.

To Bob Goff – from the time I first heard you speak at NPCC, I was captivated by your energy and lavish ways you love others. In 2018 (late to the party) when I read the ending to Love Does, it affirmed in my heart what I imagined was possible for this book. Thank you for inspiring me to dream big.

To everyone who has supported my creative business – without realizing it at the time, the writing experience I've gained in that endeavor, like blogging, social posts, and website copy, laid the foundation for writing this book. I have you to thank for that.

Confession: I want to include every person I've been lucky enough to know (including small group friends!), because our lives are shaped by the people in them. If we've crossed paths, you're a part of this, too. I'm grateful for you.

And to you, dear reader – you have my unending gratitude for diving deep into the stories of La Casa de mi Padre, and spreading love in the process.

Notes

Chapter 1: Earthquake

1   Govt. El Salvador, "El Salvador: Recovery plan from the damage caused by the earthquakes of Jan 13th & Feb 13th, 2001," March 7,2001, https://reliefweb.int/report/el-salvador/el-salvador-recovery-plan-dam-age-caused-earthquakes-jan-13th-feb-13th-2001/.

2   Joshua 1:9.

Chapter 2: Eyes Adjusting

3   "Explore All Countries – El Salvador," The World Factbook, https://www.cia.gov/the-world-factbook/countries/el-salvador/.

Chapter 3: Moving Day

4   The Autobiography of George Müller (Gideon House Books: 2017), Kindle version.

5   "Gringo" is a term many Central Americans use to refer to people from the United States. It's not necessarily meant to be offensive.

6   Matthew 14:29.

Chapter 4: Fish and Loaves

7   Matthew 14:13–21.

Chapter 5: The Miracle Farm

8   Puschel's website – http://puschel.holmer.info/.

9   Just two months before I published this book, I learned that Puschel's parents had written their own book sharing stories from their daughter's life. Many of Puschel's own journal entries from her time in El Salvador and during her illness are shared inside the book. It's there I learned

about her website and the bell recording. In reading the book, Puschel's faith has impacted me deeply, even though we never had the chance to meet. I encourage you to read about her life, as well.

Johannes and Eva-Maria Holmer, I Know God's Plan is Perfect: Lydia a Life Full of Trust (Johannes Holmer: 2022), Kindle version, 114-115 (bell story).

Chapter 8: Sting
10   https://eagleranch.org/about-us/wings-initiative/.

Chapter 9: Hope
11   Matthew 10:39.

Chapter 10: Grace
12   José L. González, Machismo Y Matriarcado [Machismo and Matriarchy] (Semilla: 2015), 31.

Chapter 11: Breaking and Revealing
13   Sharon actually said, "Fifty-six." Fifty-six is the number most often recalled by those at La Casa. However, documentation in my research showed the accurate number is fifty-nine.

Chapter 12: Horse Healing
14   https://berich.org/.
15   1 Timothy 6:17–18.

Chapter 14: A Different Future
16   InsideOut is the high school environment of North Point Ministries. https://northpoint.org/insideout/.

Chapter 17: Better Together
17   https://globalx.org/.

Chapter 18: Joy
18   https://maestrocares.org/about-us/.
19   https://www.shaws.com.sv/.

About the Author

Christina Steward is a writer and artist who serves with La Casa de mi Padre as often as she can. She's spent years doing creative things like blogging, drawing, painting, metalsmithing, and knitting. NBC even displayed her charcoal artwork on the set of 'Parenthood'. She was formerly a software developer, loves to read, check off lists, and snarf chocolate. Christina and her husband, Chad, live near Atlanta.

For more information visit christinasteward.com.

Made in the USA
Columbia, SC
20 September 2022

67656679R00114